DISTRIBUTIST PERSPECTIVES

VOLUME II

IN GRATITUDE TO MARY PENTY

A Daughter, loyal, both to her Catholic Faith
and to the memory and work of her illustrious father,
Arthur Joseph Penty, Distributist and Social Critic.

Distributist Perspectives

Volume II

Essays on the Economics of Justice and Charity

Eric Gill • Dorothy Sayers • Viscount Lymington
H. J. Massingham • H. Robbins • K. L. Kenrick
Philip Hagreen • George Maxwell • S. Sagar
Jorian Jenks • H. D. C. Pepler

With an Introduction by Allan Carlson, Ph.D.

IHS PRESS
Non est enim potestas nisi a Deo

Norfolk, VA
2008

Distributist Perspectives Volume II.

Essays by Pepler, Jenks, Sagar, Maxwell, Hagreen, Kenrick, and Robbins are included thanks to the courtesy and generosity of Aidan Mackey, whose collection of original publications were put at the Press's disposal for the purposes of this and future anthologies. The respective authors' Estates hold copyrights to "Education for What?," by Eric Gill, "Cottagers," by H. J. Massingham, and "How Free Is the Press?," by Dorothy Sayers; the latter was made available through the kind permission of David Higham Associates.

Notes to the original texts are included as footnotes. Editor's notes have been included as endnotes and are therefore to be found at the back of this edition, immediately following the texts and just prior to the biographical sketches.

ISBN-13: 978-1-932528-12-1
ISBN-10: 1-932528-12-1

Library of Congress Cataloging-in-Publication Data

Distributist perspectives / [compiled by John Sharpe ... [et al.]].
p. cm.
Subtitle varies.
ISBN-13: 978-1-932528-12-1
1. Distributive justice. 2. Wealth--Moral and ethical aspects. I. Sharpe, John, 1971-
HB523.D568 2003
330—dc21

2003005883

Printed in the United States of America.

IHS Press is the only publisher dedicated exclusively to the social teachings of the Catholic Church. For more information, contact:

IHS Press
222 W. 21st St., Suite F-122
Norfolk, VA 23517
info@ihspress.com
www.ihspress.com
877-IHS-PRESS

Table of Contents

"We hear much of a new knowledge of Medievalism and of a Medieval revival. This is far more than a question of architectural style, more than an escape from contemporary imperialism into the free democracy of the Middle Ages, more than a restoration of the Medieval industrial system. It is in effect a return to the religion and the philosophy of the Catholic ages, which made possible Gothic art and the guild system and the social unit of human scale.

"The world is ready for the great return."

—Ralph Adams Cram
New York, 1918

Introduction

THE MID 1940s PRODUCED A NEW BURST OF DISTRIBUTIST writing and optimism over a possible Distributist future. Even global war gave rise to thoughts and dreams of a world rebuilt on the principles of widely distributed property and renewed family and community life. Although the work of the great apostles of Distributism, G. K. Chesterton and Hilaire Belloc, lay in the recent past, Distributist ideals still inspired prominent and able writers, who found a ready audience.

In the United States, the Distributist journal *Free America* continued to publish during World War II, albeit as a quarterly rather than a monthly. American Distributists, or "decentralists" as they sometimes preferred, actually saw the war as a fresh opportunity for the application of their ideas. Lewis Mumford urged that wartime social planning seek "to establish every new industry, every new highway, every new housing development with the new regional pattern of decentralization." Peter Van Dresser pointed to economic decentralization as the best defense against blitzkrieg and aerial bombing. Stringfellow Barr called for a "world republic" built on small, regional entities, arguing that "[d]ecentralists and agrarians ought most surely to be in the ranks of those who have discovered the TNT concealed in national sovereignty." Herbert Agar, the founder of *Free America* and a former editor at *G. K.'s Weekly*, cast the war as a contest between a "super-industrializing" Germany and the Allies fighting "for a chance for decent men and women to live their lives without cruelty . . . . They wanted to be left alone, to tend their gardens and look after their businesses . . . . "

In early 1945, the Pulitzer-prize winning novelist Louis Bromfield published *Pleasant Valley*, an account of his creation of Malabar Farm on 700 acres in Ohio. The writer aimed at building a self-sufficient, agricultural mecca, an association of families working cooperatively, a community that would lure others back to the land. To counter the growth of "great mechanized farms," Bromfield sought "a way to operate a big farm without displacing families." The book attracted a huge readership, particularly among young men serving in the armed forces, who yearned for a return to the land at war's end, and who found inspiration in Bromfield's "romantic" report.

However, by 1950, these Distributist dreams had all but vanished on American soil. The mechanization of American agriculture, already encouraged by wartime labor shortages, actually accelerated with the coming of peace. Men trained to use modern machines in war, it appears, would not go back to mules or to a team of horses. The farm population began a steady decline. The 250 subsistence homestead projects created through Federal government subsidy during the 1930's were cut off; tract suburban housing on small lots became the favored postwar form of habitation. *Free America* ceased publication in early 1947, its editors clearly divided over the future. Some, such as the last managing editor John P. Chamberlain, turned toward an anti-statist libertarianism; others, such as Agar, found hope in Scandinavian social democracy. "Distributism seems to be a casualty of the war," Chamberlain concluded. Louis Bromfield also abandoned the cause. His 1948 book, *Malabar Farm*, dismissed his 1945 dreams. "The pattern of the general farm" and "the pattern of self-sufficiency" had "outlived" their usefulness, he now reported. Mechanization, gains from specialization, and new science made industrialized agriculture the imperative. The farmer of the future would not be the head of a family living on its land and relying on its own labor, but rather "a businessman, a specialist and something of a scientist."

This new collection of essays, covering the years 1943–48, might be counted as the last great flowering of Distributist dreams in England before the curious sleep of the 1950s set in. The majority appeared in two journals, *The Weekly Review* and *The Cross and the Plough*, and they offer new articulations of familiar Distributist themes. For example, the artist and writer Eric Gill takes issue with a system of schooling centered on careers, urging instead "a truly religious education" focused on the child's "ultimate heavenly destiny." The novelist and playwright Dorothy Sayers exposes the unfree nature of a "free press" dependent on advertising and the whims of "Press Lords." In an extraordinary extract from his 1943 book, *Alternative to Death*, The Earl of Portsmouth, Viscount Lymington, stresses the need for human lives to be in harmony with Nature: "We calculate our children with contraceptives but omit to make the wholeness of environment and love which is home." Only "ruralization" can preserve human civilization, he insists, for it is the true home of the bountiful family. Farm and fertility go together:

> The soil decrees the unit of the family; since, except for the infant, each member fits into his or her place for livelihood . . . . If the family is the natural unit for the organization of the husbandman, his work should teach him the importance of his function as a procreator.

The preservation of subsistence homesteads remained a key Distributist goal. "Cottagers" by H.J.Massingham exposes the ways in which the British government suppressed small holding agriculture and subsistence husbandry, most recently through the War Agriculture Committee. Harold Robbins reminds his countrymen that it has been "the image of an English village" that has inspired them in times of war. Even in 1947, "the village, battered, starved and abused, has survived because it is essential to the only thing stronger than industrialism," namely "the life of the land." Like most true

Distributists, Robbins condemns the suburban environment as worse than that of the city. Hilary Pepler, meanwhile, offers a stirring defense of a vanishing English institution: Common Land, set aside for communitarian ends.

The import of craftsmanship also receives new iterations here. Philip Hagreen contributes a fine essay on the examples of St. Joseph and Jesus as skilled carpenters. They produced items to meet "the normal needs of the neighborhood," using "raw material, the wood, [that] was local." They owned their own tools and applied "the practical intelligence" of their craft to make items that "were works of art." Hagreen goes on to condemn those contemporary Church leaders who have failed to confront the evils of industrialism and to embrace and defend true "craft." George Maxwell underscores how "the dustman," or waste collector, can know true dignity of labor in an economy rightly oriented toward nature. Jorian Jenks restates the old Distributist truth that food raised on small family homesteads is more wholesome, tasty, and healthy than processed foods treated as commodities.

Greater theoretical precision was another Distributist goal. In 1946, S. Sagar authored an extended essay on Distributism which captures the sense of new opportunity briefly experienced in the post-war years. "The time is ripe" for a restatement of Distributist goals, he reports, above all: "Family ownership in the means of production so widely distributed as to be the mark of the economic life of the community – that is the Distributist's desire." Sagar also points to the "sham fight between those blood brothers, Capitalism and Socialism," a Distributist theme also taken up by K. L. Kendrick's "Man's Conquest of Nature."

By 1950, though, the Cold War was in full swing, as were the suburbanization of England and the rapid growth of the welfare state (what Belloc called, more accurately, "the servile state"). As in America, Distributism retreated from the public stage, a seeming irrelevance in an age given over to the cult of the "big": big industry, big labor, big agriculture, and big government.

Yet this world faced its own crisis, starting sometime in the 1960's, as the internal contradictions of these lumbering institutions emerged. Scattered thinkers began to resurrect the "third way" of Distributism as a true alternative to "those blood brothers, Capitalism and Socialism," both of which embraced industrial organization and a post-family order.

This volume, as earlier ones from IHS Press, testifies to the profound relevance of Distributist ideas to our early 21st Century world. Bloated governments, tumbling birthrates, bankrupt or vanished factories, and the dismal reality of low-wage jobs in a "service economy" show that Chesterton, Belloc, and their intellectual allies and heirs truly understood how the world works. Although sixty years old, these essays speak directly to our age. And they provide more than theory. Indeed, they point to alternative ways of living, learning, and working that are in harmony with human nature, including the home school, the home garden, the craftsman's shop, the religiously-inspired community, and the necessary human bond to a place on earth.

Allan Carlson
Rockford, Illinois
June 5. 2008
St. Boniface

The Water Gate at the end of Essex Street in London; etching by Edgar Holloway (b. 1914).

Holloway was taught engraving by Phillip Hagreen (1890–1988) at Ditchling in 1948, where he moved permanently with his family a year later. In 1951 he joined the Guild of St. Joseph and St. Dominic.

The Distributist League, *G. K.'s Weekly*, and its successor papers *The Weekly Review* and *The Register* all had Essex Street addresses, and the first League meeting took place there in Essex Hall on September 17, 1926.

I
Education for What?
by Eric Gill

WHAT IS THE GENERAL OBJECT AND END OF EDUcation? Obviously, you cannot lead a person in a way unnatural to him. When you teach, bring up, train a horse, it is always remembered that it is a horse you are dealing with. We do not try anything else. But with human beings we are much more muddled. It seems as though we hardly know what human beings are or what they are for. Yet, obviously, that is the first thing to find out. What is a human being? What end is he made for?

In the world today, whatever we say about it, we act almost entirely as though human beings had no reason for being except to *get on* in the world–to acquire a lot of material possessions–to get a good paying job. That seems to be considered the first and most important thing. On top of that we think it would be a good thing if people had a sort of ornamental veneer of culture and good manners–that they be able to appreciate good books and to speak with a refined accent.

This ambition of parents to give children such an education as will enable them to *get on* and get *a good job* is obviously due to a certain view of what a human being is. Whatever we may *say*, we *act* as though a human being was simply a creature, an animal, whose sole job it was to earn his living, acquire ample means to live comfortably, and then pass out. This seems to be the sole object of existence of other animals, and we seem to think that man is only an animal among animals. The only

* *This chapter is taken from "Education for What?," Chapter 18 of* It All Goes Together: Selected Essays *(New York; The Devin-Adair Company, 1944), pp. 135–41.*

difference between man and other animals seems to be that whereas other animals reproduce their kind to the utmost of their powers and without consideration of their *own* comfort or convenience, men and women, on the other hand, though they have as strong an instinct for mating as other animals, do not proceed in this matter unselfishly or without regard to their own comfort and convenience. And so we find that the more successful we are in the pursuit of riches, the more we *get on* and get rich, so much the more we think of our comfort and so much the more we restrict our families. Perhaps other animals would do the same if they had more wits. But they do not, and so it seems that the main difference between man and other animals is that men are cleverer and more cunning and more self-regarding and *more selfish*, and that our desire for culture and good manners is bound up with *getting on*; for the better your manners, the more likely you are to beat your more boorish competitors, and the more proofs you can show of having learnt poetry and foreign languages, so much the more will you outshine your fellows.

So it seems that today our definition of man is: That he is an animal who exists in order to enjoy himself while he lives, and therefore the object of education is to draw out all those faculties which are suitable to that end. First of all, he must learn how to acquire a good living, and, secondly, how to enjoy it in the manner least likely to endanger it. We must learn how to acquire riches and we must learn not to squander them in riotous living. Shorn of all camouflage, that represents the general line of people's ideas today. That is not what we *say*, but it is how we *act*. And even the more *highbrow* people are really acting in the same way; for though, perhaps, they say that the object of education is to draw out the very best that is in us–to teach us to know ourselves and control ourselves so that we may enjoy ourselves even more–it all comes to the same thing–to acquire the means to live well and then to enjoy life. For, after all, the saying "Eat, drink and be merry," depends upon its interpretation. It does not necessarily mean eat and drink as much as possible, but eat and drink as much as will enable you to be merry. And being merry does not necessarily mean buffoonery and horseplay and drunken revelry; it may mean the most refined high-art enjoyments. So whether we are *highbrows* or *lowbrows*, the definition of man which is accepted today comes to the same thing: in either case it means that we have no idea of man except that his only reason for existence is to get on in this world and have as good a time as possible.

*****

PERHAPS THERE are two chief causes of this rather limited view of man:

1. The decay and disappearance of unity in religion; and

2. The tremendous growth of the power and prestige of the commercial world.

But perhaps these two things are two sides of the same thing; for where religion is strong, commerce is always weak. So perhaps we may say that the one and only cause of our limited and materialistic view of man is the decay of religious unity, for where there are a hundred rival sects there cannot be power. The devil may well approve of the military rule, *Divide and conquer.* For where, instead of one religion swaying the hearts and minds of men, there are a hundred rival religions, it is obvious that no one of them can be really powerful, and no one of them can unite us all together and inspire us.

There is no need for me to say here which, if any, of the rival religions is, in my opinion, the true one. I am only pointing out that, in the absence of religious unity, the one and only thing which can unite men is the desire of material riches. Religion, they now say, is your private affair–nothing to do with how the state is run–nothing to do with how you earn your living–nothing to do with your work.

But if the common materialistic view of man leaves much to be desired–and few people are really satisfied with it–it is obviously a very limited view and takes no account of those qualities in men which we all agree to admire most: humility, unselfishness, tenderness, except insofar as they help us to *get on*–and it takes no account of the quite common appetite of men for something real and unchanging and not liable to decay and death–I say, if the common materialistic definition of man leaves much to be desired, what other view is there? If man is not just an animal among animals, what is he? Well, I think, even without entering into the awful field of religious controversy, we may say certain things. God exists; He is a Person–the Personal Author and Ruler of all things. *And we are His people and the sheep of His pasture.* And we are made in His image–that is to say, we share in God's spiritual nature. We are rational beings and can deliberate and weigh the pros and cons of action; and having thus weighed, we can act freely. Whether or no we can do good of ourselves, we can certainly refrain from evil, even if we are to some extent–perhaps to a large extent–the victims of our physical and psychological *make-up.* We are, therefore, rightly held to be *responsible persons* and not automata obeying willy-nilly the forces to which we find ourselves subjected. And if we are thus children of God–for we are, in this religious view of man, more than just animals without responsibility (after all, you can punish a dog–but you cannot really *blame* him)–if we are children of God, then we are heirs also. We are called to some sort of sharing with God in His own life. We have what we call a *vocation.* We have, in fact, a destiny independent of our physical life on this earth. A destiny for which this physical life is a training ground and place of preparation. It is, in fact, a school–a place where we are *educated.*

It is clear then, is it not? that if we accept the religious view of man's nature, we are compelled to take a very different, a radically different view of education. No longer can we think merely of *getting on* in the commercial and materialistic sense. We must now think of getting on in the sense of getting heavenwards. And in everything we learn and in everything we teach to our children or our pupils, we must bear this fact in mind. We must learn to get on in the world–not as an end in itself, but as a means to getting heavenwards. Any education which neglects this fact, and to the extent to which it neglects it, is false education, because it is false to man. It is untrue; it is not in accordance with his nature as a child of God and heir also.

All this sounds very pious – though there is no harm in that and some people will think that I am advocating an almost total neglect of practical things – that perhaps I despise worldly success, that I despise reading, writing, and arithmetic and dancing and gymnastics and science and history. That is not so. What I am saying is simply that as parents and teachers we must teach these things with *an eye on our goal.* If, like the materialists, and that is, in practice, most people today, we think there is no goal, then of course, there is nothing to be said against that kind of education which has for its sole object the training of children to win prizes and get good jobs, and we should then approve of the London County Council (L.C.C.) which says in its advertisements of its evening classes:

> *Turn your energy into pounds, shillings, and pence. L.C.C. Evening Classes offer a good return on your investment.*

and we should approve of our men of business, who see everything in terms of money – who think that the production of dividends is the first object of industrial enterprise (as the Railway Stockholders' Union says: *British Railways are in business to earn dividends*); for to the man of business, the only criterion of what is good is what will sell.

But if we do not accept the materialist philosophy, if we do not agree with the economic interpretation of history, if we do not think man is nothing more than a creature made for gaining material wealth, if we take the religious point of view – because, if we think for half a moment, we know that we are not satisfied working merely to make money to buy things which have been made by people who only made them in order to sell them . . . then we shall take a radically different view of education.

We shall even take a radically different view of arithmetic and of reading and writing–because we shall attack them in a totally different frame of mind. That is the point. It is not that we shall do nothing but write hymns, though the best poems are hymns. It is not that we shall only read the Bible, though the Bible is the best book, or that we shall only count how much we can give away (instead of counting how much we can spend), it is simply that we shall see all things as in some way heavenly or leading heavenwards. For education will not then mean drawing out those faculties which make us successful worldlings, but drawing out those faculties which make us better fitted for an eternal rather than a merely temporary existence. We shall see everything, as the philosopher says, *sub specie aeternitatis*–that is to say we shall see everything *in its real shape*, its eternal shape, the shape of its *being* rather than the shape of its *doing*. For it is not what we *do* that matters most, but what we *are*. And it is the same with things as with persons. Being is more important than doing. But if, like the materialists and their followers, the businessmen of today, we say there is no being behind doing, but only doing, then we shall not only lose the Kingdom of God in heaven but also the Kingdom of God on earth. Newport and Swansea, Birmingham and the Black Country, Manchester, Glasgow, the wilds of east and south-east London! What could be more ungodly? And what could more plainly be the proper reward of our greed and avarice and our refusal to educate ourselves and our children except to *get on* or *get out*? And the *war, pestilence, and famine*, which are upon us, what are they but the due reward of our sins?

But in spite of our enthusiasm for worldly success, we all know that a worldly view of education is very unsatisfactory–to say the least. It does not satisfy us. We want something more. And very often we think that all will be well if, in addition to learning things which will be useful to enable us to *get on*, we add what we call *cultured subjects*–a spot of *art*, a spot of poetry and foreign languages, just in the same way as people build banks and town halls with iron frames and concrete and all the cheapest and most labour-saving methods, and then cover the front with elaborate stonework in imitation of a classical temple, with columns and carvings.

So we think that children should have *a good, sound practical education*, which will enable them to make money – that is the iron and concrete part – and that then they should have culture – that is the pillars and carvings on the front. We all know those buildings (they are everywhere), which have fine imitation Queen Anne or Gothic or Classic fronts and then when you go into the backyard you see only white glazed bricks and drain pipes – as someone said: *Queen Anne fronts and Mary Anne backs*. But we can easily see that this is all nonsense; for if we cannot make our building fine and noble and beautiful all through, front and back and inside and out, then it would be much better, more honest and more holy, to confine ourselves to the Mary Anne part alone, and see how truly well and nobly we can do the drains and the drain-pipes, and leave out the sham architecture.

And so it is with education. If we cannot give our children a truly religious education, through and through, so that everything they learn is in harmony with their ultimate heavenly destiny, then it would be much better if we confined ourselves to the plain bread-and-butter part of the business and simply taught them practical things – the three R's and physical jerks and how to read a Bradshaw[1] and drive a car – and leave out the classics and Shakespeare and all the sham culture.

For culture is a sham if it is only a sort of Gothic front put on an iron building – like the Tower Bridge – or a classical front put on a steel frame – like the *Daily Telegraph* building in Fleet Street. Culture, if it is to be a real thing and a holy thing, must be the product of what we actually do for a living – not something added, like sugar on a pill.

So it all comes back to this: What is man? Is he just an animal for whom earthly life is all? Or is he a Child of God with eternal life in view?

II
How Free Is the Press?

by Dorothy L. Sayers

THAT WITHOUT A FREE PRESS THERE CAN BE NO free people is a thing that all free peoples take for granted; we need not discuss it. Nor will we at this moment discuss the restrictions placed upon the Press in time of war. At such times all liberties have to be restricted; a free people must see to it that when peace comes full freedom is restored. In the meantime, it may be wholesome to consider what that freedom is, and how far it is truly desirable. It may turn out to be no freedom at all, or even a mere freedom to tyrannise; for tyranny is, in fact, the uncontrolled freedom of one man, or one gang, to impose its will on the world.

When we speak of "the freedom of the Press," we usually mean freedom in a very technical and restricted sense – namely, freedom from direction or censorship by the Government. In this respect, the British Press is, under ordinary conditions, singularly free. It can attack the policy and political character of ministers, interfere in the delicate machinery of foreign diplomacy, conduct campaigns to subvert the Constitution, incite citizens to discontent and rebellion, expose scandals and foment grievances, and generally harry and belabour the servants of the State, with almost perfect liberty. On occasion, it can become a weapon to coerce the Government to conform to what it asserts to be the will of the people.

So far, this is all to the good. Occasionally, this freedom may produce disastrous hesitations and inconsistencies in

* *This chapter is taken from "How Free is the Press?" from* Unpopular Opinions *(London: Victor Gollancz, 1946), pp. 127–133.*

public policy, or tend to hamper the swift execution of emergency measures; but, generally speaking, it works to secure and sustain that central doctrine of Democracy as we understand it—that the State is not the master but the servant of the people.

The Press, *as a whole*, and in this technical and restricted sense, is thus pretty free in a peaceful Britain. There is no shade of political opinion that does not somehow contrive to express itself. But if we go on to imagine that *any particular organ* of the Press enjoys the larger liberty of being a "forum of public opinion," we are gravely mistaken. Every newspaper is shackled to its own set of overlords and, in its turn, like the Unmerciful Servant, exercises a powerful bondage upon its readers and on the public generally. Indeed, we may say that the heaviest restriction upon the freedom of public opinion is not the official censorship *of* the Press, but the unofficial censorship *by* a Press which exists not so much to express opinion as to manufacture it.

The editorial policy of a popular daily is controlled by two chief factors. The first is the interest of the advertisers from whom it gets the money which enables it to keep up its large circulation. No widely circulated newspaper dare support a public policy, however much in the national interest, that might conflict with the vested interests of its advertisers. Thus, any proposal to control the marketing of branded goods (as, for example, of margarine in 1939) will be violently opposed, on the loftiest hygienic grounds, by the papers that carry the branded advertising. On the other hand, any product that refuses to pay the high advertising rates of a powerful national organ will be (again on the highest moral and hygienic grounds) denounced, smashed, and driven off the market; you are not allowed to use any product that dissociates itself from the advertising ring. All this is understandable, since a big circulation spells bankruptcy if the paper has to depend on its sales for its revenue. Every newspaper lives in a perpetual precarious balance: it *must* increase its sales to justify its advertising rates, and to increase its sales, it *must* sell itself far below the cost of production; but if it sells more copies than its advertising will pay for, it faces financial disaster. Consequently, the more widespread and powerful the organ, the more closely it has to subserve vested interests.

This means that the cheap daily paper, which goes everywhere and has most influence, is far less free than the more expensive weekly or monthly, which draws a higher proportion of its revenue from sales. Therefore it is only the comparatively rich who can afford to read independent expressions of opinion.

The second chief source of a newspaper's revenue is the wealth of the man or company that owns it; accordingly, its policy is largely determined by the personal spites and political ambitions of its proprietor. The failure, for example, of a great newspaper magnate to secure a government appointment may be the signal for the unleashing of a virulent campaign, in every organ which he controls, against the minister or the party which has disappointed his ambitions. The public, knowing nothing of the personal bias behind the attack and little of the vast network of control which ties up whole groups of the London and Provincial Press in the hands of a single man or combine, sees only that great numbers of (what appear to him to be) independent organs are united in a single, savage and persistent condemnation. Unless he is exceptionally shrewd, exceptionally cynical, or of exceptionally resolute and independent mind, he can scarcely help being influenced, and having his vote influenced; and it is odds that he will never realize the nature of the pressure brought to bear upon him.

But still more serious, because more subtle, than the control applied to individual papers by various kinds of interest is the control and censorship exercised by the Press upon the news and opinions which it disseminates. This control rests upon and exploits two basic assumptions about the public—(a) that they have not the wit to distinguish truth from falsehood; (b) that they do not care at all that a statement is false, provided it is titillating. Neither assumption is flattering; and indeed, between the language used privately by the late Lord Northcliffe[2] about his British readers and the language used publicly by Hitler about his German readers there is very little to choose. Both assume that readers can be made to believe anything. The result is that accurate reporting, which used to be the pride of the old-fashioned independent newspaper, has largely given place to reporting which is at best slipshod and at worst tendentious.

I should like to illustrate, with quite trivial examples drawn from personal experience, the curious ways by which both fact and opinion can be distorted, so that a kind of smear of unreality is spread over the whole newspaper page, from reports of public affairs down to the most casual items of daily gossip.

1. *Sensational Headline: False Emphasis: and Suppression of Context.* This year–1941–at the Malvern Conference, I read a paper dealing with the theological grounds for the Church's concern with politics and sociology, with the complementary dangers of Pietism[3] and Caesarism, and with the importance of Incarnation doctrine in this connection. Out of 8,000 words, some 250 dealt with the connection between Caesarism and an undue emphasis placed on sexual, as contrasted with financial, morality. This quite subsidiary paragraph was reported everywhere, under sensational headlines, in such a manner as to convey that this passing allusion formed the whole subject-matter of my address. Out of the 8,000 words about theology, the reporters picked the only one which they presumed their readers capable of understanding–to wit, "fornication." You, the reader, will appreciate the compliment. I will, however, add for your comfort that this report was not made (as you might well suppose) by a Pressman from your favourite paper, specially selected for his understanding of ecclesiastical affairs. All the distorted reports emanated from a News Agency; and the individual editors, when remonstrated with, were for the most part content to disavow responsibility. This is how you learn what happens at public meetings.

2. *Garbling.* This is the special accomplishment of the Press interviewer. During the production of my latest play, I was asked, "What were my plans for the future?" I replied that I never made plans; that I preferred writing plays to novels, though novels paid better; and that, financial considerations notwithstanding, if the opportunity to write a play were to present itself–for example, another commission for the Canterbury Festival[4]–I should undoubtedly write it. This reply duly appeared in the Press, in the form: "Miss Sayers said she would write no more plays, except on commission."

Bland perversions of this kind, together with the interviewer's playful habit of making statements himself and attributing them to his victim, make reported interviews singularly unreliable reading. (One most allow for the Pressman's vivid imagination. I remember reading with interest that my eyes "glittered behind my glass" when making some remark or other; since that particular interview was given by telephone, I could only conclude that the interviewer's own eyes must have been "double-magnifying gas microscopes of extra power.") But the last, best word on Press interviews has been written by "Q" in *From a Cornish Window;*[5] those who believe that public characters say everything they are reported as saying should read it and take warning.

3. *Inaccurate Reporting of Facts.* Some time ago a daily paper reported that my flat had been broken into the previous day, and that I had returned from (I think they said) Oxford, in time to disturb the thieves. This was true enough, *except* that every detail was wrong. The date was three days earlier than alleged, I was not at Oxford but at the King's Garden Party, and the intruders had been disturbed, not by me, but most likely by the newspaper boy. The interest here lies in the probable reasons for the mis-statements. The date had to be changed to conceal the fact that the news was already "cold;" and I was substituted for the boy, presumably for my greater snob-value. The altered date was a bad blunder–Buckingham Palace would have adorned the tale to so much better advantage.

4. *Plain Reversal of the Facts.* On a summons for unshaded lights, a letter of mine was read to the Bench explaining that my servant had carefully drawn the curtains, but that there had proved, unfortunately, to be a defect in the curtains themselves. The local paper duly reported: "Miss Sayers said that a servant had forgotten to draw the curtains." (This was calculated to cause pain and distress to my servant–but why should anybody care?)

5. *Random Gratuitous Invention.* Without consulting me at all, a small and gossipy paper recently informed its readers that two of my favourite hobbies were "gardening and keeping cats." I do not see why anybody should want to know my hobbies–but if they do it would surely be better to mention the right ones. This choice was peculiarly unfortunate. If there is anything I detest, it is gardening; and although my household always includes a necessary cat, which lives in the kitchen and is supposed to catch mice, I have little to do with it, except to remove it and its hairs from the chairs and cushions, and open the door for it from time to time under protest.*

6. *Deliberate Miracle-Mongering.* It was recently reported in various local papers that, in a public address, I had delivered some 20,000 words in the space of an hour and a quarter. This would in any case have been impossible. Actually, the reporter *had had the full text of my speech in his hands*, and could have seen for himself that it consisted of almost exactly 8,000 words. The error was thus precisely 150 per cent., a useful figure on which to base one's estimate of truth in reporting.

Of these six main forms of misrepresentation, the first two are the most dangerous. There is no remedy against them. They do not come within the narrow range of the law of libel; for to misrepresent a man's attitude and opinions is no offence. Nor could one readily persuade a jury that a lie had been told about one, since a sort of formal veracity *in detail* is used to convey a

---

*Shortage of domestic staff has since constrained me to live on more intimate terms with the cat. But if he is a "hobby", then so are the handy-man and the "daily woman."

totally false impression of the speaker's words *as a whole*. Consequently, it is next door to impossible to secure either correction or apology. Which brings us to:

7. *Flat Suppression*. Letters of protest may be written. These may be (a) ignored; (b) printed in full or in part, accompanied by an editorial comment to the effect that the words reported were actually said, and that the speaker must not expect to monopolise the whole of the paper's valuable space; (c) answered privately by the editor–a manoeuvre that does nothing to correct the false impression left in the public mind. Only occasionally, and usually from a provincial paper, does one receive full apology and correction. Let me quote *honoris causa*, a note written to me from an editor of the older school: "Thank you for your letter, which we thought it our duty to print–we try to preserve our reputation for balanced news." Here are three old-fashioned words, *duty, balance, reputation*: do they still represent what the reader demands, or expects from Fleet Street?

To get misleading statements corrected entails, in any case, heavy and exhausting effort of correspondence–for the falsehood may be syndicated all over the world overnight and appear simultaneously in several hundred papers. In addition, if one makes a fuss, or ventures to accuse the newspapers of lack of veracity, there always lurks in the background the shadow of a genteel blackmail. Any public person–writer, speaker, actor, politician–is subtly made to feel that if he offends the Press he will suffer for it.

No threat, of course, is openly uttered; but books and plays may be unfavourably noticed or silently ignored–allusions sneering, though not actually libellous, may crop up in the gossip columns–a thousand hints will be quietly conveyed that the Press can make or break reputations. Books which venture to criticise the Press are therefore rare; nor is it easy to find a paper honest enough to print an article on the subject.

Speeches may be made, of course, but they will not reach the wider public, for they will not be reported in full; only a carefully isolated sentence or so will find its way into the papers, under some such headline as: "Bishop Seeks to Muzzle Press," or "M.P. Attacks Press Liberty." Indeed, the slightest effort to hinder the irresponsible dissemination of nonsense is greeted by a concerted howl: "This is a threat to the Freedom of the Press!"

No wonder that within three days lately the Archbishop of York and a Minister of the Crown were heard to utter the same despairing cry in face of journalistic misrepresentation and indiscretion: "We cannot control the Press!"

The particular examples I have given are, you will say, of very small importance. True: that is what makes them so symptomatic and so disquieting. They do not show any direct wresting of the truth towards a propagandist end–against such attempts the reader may, with a little mental effort, efficiently arm himself. What they do clearly show is an all-pervading carelessness about veracity, penetrating every column, creeping into the most trifling item of news, smudging and blurring the boundary lines between fact and fancy, creating a general atmosphere of cynicism and mistrust.

He that is unfaithful in little is unfaithful also in much; if a common court case cannot be correctly reported, how are we to believe the reports of world events? If an interviewer misinterprets the novelist whom we have all seen, what does he do with the foreign statesman whom we have never seen? If the papers can be convicted of False Emphasis, Garbling, Inaccuracy, Reversal of the Fact, Random Invention, Miracle-Mongering and Flat Suppression in cases where such distortions are of advantage to nobody, what are we to suppose about those cases in which vested interests are closely concerned? And, above all, what are we to make of the assumptions on which all this is based–that the reader is too stupid to detect falsehood and too frivolous even to resent it?

Decent journalists do not like the present state of affairs. Nor do the more responsible editors. But the number of editors and journalists who can maintain a high standard of "duty, balance, and reputation" in the face of pressure grows less day by day. It is difficult for any paper that presents its news soberly to maintain its circulation: perhaps it is true that every nation gets the Press it deserves.

But supposing the reader does care about accuracy, does resent contempt for his intelligence, does want the truth about what is said and done—what steps is he to take? How is he to get at the facts which are withheld; or smothered under these mountains of distortion and absurdity? How is he to make his will felt? Is he to write angry letters, or transfer his daily penny from one organ to another? Will anybody care if he does? They will care if he protests in sufficient numbers. But his penny is a small weapon to oppose against the vested interests and the pooled money of the great combines. His helplessness is a measure of the freedom which the Press enjoys—but is the reader free?

The common man has a vote in Parliament. He has a Parliamentary representative whom he can badger and heckle and whose tenure of office rests upon his consent. If he likes to make use of the machinery of a democracy, he can have questions asked in the House; in the last resort, he can destroy one government and make another. But there is no machinery by which he can control the organs which mould opinion. For that, his sole resource is a penny a day and his native wit and will. In time of crisis, the newspapers are first with the cry: "Let the people know the Facts!" But perhaps Fact is a deity invoked by the people only in the last emergency when the easy gods of peace have failed them.

III
Nature, the Family, and the Nation
by Viscount Lymington

When McCarrison[6] discovered that rats fed on the equivalent diet of many of our city dwellers grew diseased, nervous, treacherous, quarrelsome, and cannibalistic, but that similar rats fed on the fresher, whole, simple diet of some Indian hill tribes were fertile, gentle, and healthy, he thumbed a long nose at the last two centuries of "progress." His experiment diagnosed one root cause rather than the symptom of a sick world. Fresh food from well-tilled land is the basis of physical health, for earth is the matrix and the grave of our physical existence. Body, mind, and spirit in our span on the earth are one whole; thus, if we neglect the matrix, the grave alone remains the "fine and private (final) place."

History may resound to the tramp of armed men and the liberal historians may put battles down to economics and a lust for freedom: that is, licence to pursue economic gain.

But the fundamental history of civilization is the history of the soil The understanding of this is vital to all peoples who stand at the gateway of death. The whole white civilization stands there today. In any civilization there comes a moment when, if it is to continue, civilization must become ruralization. All its economics, all its amenities, its armies, and its splendour depend on one thing: the reverent use of its soil. The writing on the wall is there; we are being weighed in the balance and found wanting – in ruralization.

---

* *This chapter is taken from "Nature, The Family and The Nation," Chapter 1 of* Alternative to Death: The Relationship Between Soil, Family and Community *(London: Faber & Faber, Ltd., 1943), pp. 11–31.*

The writing is scrawled in erosion across the world. At present it goes almost unheeded; so we must return to history for proof of our present follies. Only in rare and fortunate cases does the jungle triumph and do vines choke the city walls while monkeys chatter in the roofless courts of kings. Mostly the sand and the silence drift across the crumbled splendour of man's too careless endeavours. In reasons which caused the ruins of Gobi and Sahara and the buried cities of Arabia we have more to learn for human survival than in all the chemistry, plumbing, and germ theories of today. The desert has succeeded to the cities of the past because, being cities, they bred a race which forgot the soil on which it fed. Today there are well-schooled but poorly educated children in English industrial areas who cannot believe that milk comes from the cow, and not the tin. These children had their counterparts in Rome and Nineveh.

The background of human wisdom is the ever present consciousness that the soil nourishes the plant, the plant the animal, and plant and animal the human being. Thus, the city is built from the produce of the soil. When there are too many in the city for the soil, the soil and the city perish together, as a rabbit warren is eaten bare and then poisoned by the rabbits. As soon as the soil is made the servant of the city, and not the master partner in the civilization, the desert begins. Even useless wars and gigantic wastes like the burning forests only serve to underline men's madness in forgetting their own source of life: *Quem deus perdere vult, prius dementat.*[7]

Man, insofar as he is an animal, is bound to the soil, however heaven-born he thinks himself. When he enters the city he cuts himself off from one side of his own cosmic nature, and even his fertility fails so that he has to be constantly renewed from the country stock. But the longer he remains urban bred, the more his nature is divorced from the background of human wisdom. As he develops the habits of the parasite, be he lawyer or money-changer, scribe, broker or huckster, he is fastened ever more heavily on the servant of the soil, who sinks beneath his weight. The peasant thus exploited either moves to the city to become a parasite, or else, to live, exploits the soil itself, and so with gradually increasing speed destroys his own and the parasite's source of livelihood. First the soil is exhausted of its human stock, and then of its own life-giving qualities. For many years the human exhaustion can go on, but once the exhaustion of the soil's own stores of fertility sets in, the town gives way to desert.

The fate of the Roman Empire should be our lesson. It is so curiously paralleled today: A hardy peasant stock subdues a fertile peninsula. It is a stock full of the sturdy characteristics of those who live for the soil. War kills off some of the best of that stock. War also brings opportunities to the natural parasites who congregate in the city while the battle rages outside. Already the seeds of decay are sown. Being a peninsula the sea is a natural highway leading to Empire, and above all, to trade. Trade leads to usury, and usury is to demand that money grows at the expense of living growth.

Trade for its own sake means more urban population, and successful war means an abundance of slaves. The slaves lower the market value of the free peasant's hard-won fruits of his labour. The peasant is displaced, drifting workless to the town. The *latifundia*, the large-scaled slave-worked farm, is made possible by the huge fortunes annexed through war or trade. The city population grows as the material wealth increases; conquests of corn-growing land in Africa and elsewhere are exploited by money-lenders to bring food to the city's workless, who must have bread and circuses; for if they are not drugged by uncreative amusement they are just as likely to turn against their Emperors as if they are not fed. The *latifundia* in Italy must be worked harder and harder to compete with the grain ships. All that is best in the old Empire goes to the edges where there is still a man's work to be done, and the shame of corruption at the heart is deadened by distance. Food and amusements are imported and the best go out to the perimeters to prop up a worm-ridden empire. Throughout the corruption gets worse because of the foreign customs and foreign purveyors of vices and titillating innovations which pour in to keep the capital amused, or in the form of foreign slaves to keep the now cross-bred parasites in idleness. The Barbarian sweeps over the old barriers and the dark ages succeed. But it is not the barbarian who has broken Rome, it is the neglect of the soil and its servants. The once fertile granary of Africa from the Atlas to Cyrene is a desert, and Italy is stripped bare.

Transpose this lesson to our own times: for *latifundia* and slaves read "international capitalism and mass production," for Africa read "the dust-bowl of America," for bread and circuses read "the dole, Hollywood, and the headline press." The parallel in the waste of land and the degradation of a fine yeoman stock is complete.

Reports and commissions, invention and finance will not help us if we do not remember this lesson and seek a salvation which can make integrate men; that is beings integrated within themselves and living in harmony with the whole of their environment.

I cannot believe that the Golden Age is a mere myth of superstitious ancients, or the Utopian figment of self-deceived idealists. I believe it to be a race memory, well-nigh universal of times when peoples in differing places had achieved a way of living in partnership and harmony with Nature. They possessed the secret, almost perfect, of adaptation to their environment, so that health, gentleness, beauty and strength were the rule and not the exception. That is the adaptation expressed in the Book of Job "when the morning stars sang together, and all the sons of God shouted for joy"–man conscious of his relationship to God and his unity with creation. The memory was nearer to the most ancient Egyptians and the earlier Greeks, even to the Aztecs, than to ourselves. Sometimes we may believe that there is more than a trace surviving still, when we read of the Hunzas of northern India living among the eaves of the world, or remember what Tahiti must have been before it was despoiled.

Even the story of Eden is a race memory of natural harmony and adaptation broken into by adding knowledge which could not be assimilated into wisdom. So far in this century, if we are honest with ourselves, we see that we have scientific knowledge but not the wisdom to use the knowledge to save us from shattered bodies and empty souls. We calculate our children with contraceptives but omit to make the wholeness of environment and love which is home. We are full of medical knowledge without health; scientific exploitation of the soil without the love and care, experience, and foresight to know that what we take we must return. The philosopher and the seer are at a discount, when they are most needed.

Self-knowledge must drive us to ask in humility: how may we regain a harmony with Nature†—with the ordering of life unspoiled by man's quick-tempered and unmeditative arrogance; with a pattern of life that is essentially religious, sometimes in despite of religions? Even a cursory review of legends of the Golden Age, and observation of extant survivals or historic records of healthier, fuller, and calmer ways of living, show that care for the soil and ordering of life have been fused in an almost unconscious radiance of love. Happiness born of exuberant health, nurtured by patient adherence to the common purposes are its hallmarks.

Again and again we find the story of descent from some human being transcendent in wisdom and health, transmitting his qualities to family or tribe, by whom order and tradition were established. It would be fair to say that in nearly every case one gets evidence of intense respect for the soil and its conservation, based upon the continuing close-bred life of the

† This does not mean returning to a state of Nature. Man has altered Nature for too many thousands of years for this to be possible, were it even desirable. But it does mean that we should reach a conscious understanding of our nature, instincts, and biological make-up in relation to the soil, plant, and animal life with which, and by means of which, we have to live, and that we may yet have to learn the relationship of all these matters with the solar system.

family. There is evidence also that in physical matters these happier human beings had not lost their instinct of physical adaptation to the order of Nature which may be found from the newts‡ to the felidi.[8]

On the reverse picture one gets evidence that civilization broke down because it disregarded the right use of the soil, and disintegrated because it had too much knowledge, but had lost its wisdom. We know that half the deserts of the world are monuments to human folly. The popular study of anthropology, collated with a biological knowledge of medicine and modes of agriculture, leaves us grounds for supposing that the debased savage and the cannibal were not simply laggards in the supposed race of evolution, but the relics of peoples who have taken the wrong turning earlier than ourselves. It is not difficult now to doubt the turning which our technocratic material civilization has taken in the last three hundred years. We can begin to understand how living has been divided from life, and body from spirit. When man is fragmentary and no longer integrated, it is no wonder in the endless crisis of our own disordering that men snatch at tendered panaceas–vitamin pills for the body and quack religions for the soul. We are so used to a ready-made world that many ask for a ready-made mass religion to salve their souls and even to comfort their bodies.

It is only the over-weening materialist who could flatly deny that by their approach to God the great mystics have left the human race in their debt. It is perhaps true that we need the influence of these seekers today, and that the world is parched for lack of striving after the ultimate wholeness which is assimilation into Being beyond our diurnal comprehension. But, although we may acknowledge, we cannot fulfil the need for such persons as we would apply an engineering technique to a new invention.

However, hunger for unfulfilled spiritual leadership and authority, for what we fondly believe is a short cut, should not leave us without either the energy or the faith to see that

---

‡ Professor G.E. Coghill, *Anatomy and the Problem of Behaviour.*

workaday solutions can be achieved, with the strength of purpose to work for these ends, and discipline to adhere to the values which shape them. Perhaps then, and only then, will the revived spiritual authority come to men of our day.

If we are sufficiently humble we should understand that the instinct of right living has been overlaid just as we have cast away the traditions which those instincts made.

On the other hand, however disordered our knowledge, however superficial our intellectual pride, we can still, with the power of reason and co-ordination of knowledge reproduce wisdom, and again give the best of our instinct the chance to assert itself for enduring ends. Reason, which does not apply its power for achieving harmony with Nature, or ally itself to liberating and guiding human instinct, can only plan Utopias and achieve Genevas.[9]

The chapters which follow in this book are a tentative effort to use knowledge and experience in trying to point out on practical lines some, but by no means all, of the methods which could first restore to no inconsiderable number of the English, integrity of health for body and mind, in alliance with, rather than in opposition to, Nature. My hope and belief is that these methods might make such a nucleus of sound men and women that the example and influence would grow until it embraced the whole. Therefore, before proceeding to indicate solutions, I shall have to establish the principles upon which they are to be based, and incidentally at times to refute established errors, the virtues of which are taken for granted.

I have based this book primarily on the soil; on the family; on responsibility; and the development of instinctive excellence of craft and leadership. To believe that it is possible to found and maintain a great civilization without first using, maintaining, and even enriching its soil is to court disaster—disaster due to insecurity, subnormal health, and repressed instinct. The soil is the limiting factor. It is the liberator or inhibiter of inheritance according to its quality. Breed counts, but it cannot function properly on bad or ill-used soil; only when we cherish the sources of life can sound blood fulfil its potent destiny.

If, for instance, one were to feed a well-bred race-horse on the diet of a Neapolitan cab-horse, it is unlikely that one would even get a superior cab-horse; rather an ill-tempered, ill-adapted misfit in the shafts. The nature of the soil means more than the quality of food: it affects the water we drink, the air we breathe, and the quality of the sunshine. Ill-used soil can mean bad water and unhealthy air. Science might alleviate, but could not cure these fundamental effects.

The soil constitutes our environment in the truest sense; it courses through our blood, moulds our muscle and builds our bones. It even influences our thought and characterizes our actions. I believe that we should have the humility to acknowledge that character of the soil, rather than our own convenient predilections, should determine the nature of our customs and institutions. Therefore, it should determine even the size of the population which it carries. It is an error to consider that if we could guarantee the permanent security of imports and food for all from overseas, it would bring us either health or spiritual fulfilment.

God who ordered Nature must have clearly intended that the food we eat should be as fresh as possible; just as it was intended that the wastes from that food should go back to the soil whence it comes. These are the two most obvious biological reasons why the nature of the soil should determine our institutions. There are, however, spiritual reasons as well. When men cannot see cause and effect, they forget the relationship between the two. Reverence for the soil of far countries can never be the same as reverence for the particular plot which a man may cultivate himself. Therefore, men will not care until it is too late, if the soil is abused, when they eat imported foodstuffs. This is also a most cogent argument against great cities, since the metropolitan townsman forgets that the countryside is the source of life, rather than his playground.

The soil itself is the source of responsibility in craftsmanship. It is easier to escape the consequences of bad material and scamped workmanship in mass production than in dealing with Nature. Crop and animal alike will give the lie to the scrimshanker or the second-rate, but fine workmanship and generous care receive their accolade from life. Nor can the husbandman tolerate faulty tools, however simple they may be, and so he spreads the craftsman's instinct far wider than himself. The craftsman's instinct is the foundation of culture, since it satisfies needs which must otherwise explode in barbarism. Head-hunter and gangster are substitutes for true culture. To deny the creative instinct is to enlarge the restless forces of destruction.

While the soil provides our environment, internal as well as external, it forces us to use and not abuse the instinct which makes life continue. The soil decrees the unit of the family; since, except for the infant, each member fits into his or her place for livelihood. Even the children find work which is at the same time play and school for future responsibility in the household and the field. Later, as eyes grow dim, or muscles slacken, a niche of usefulness remains. If the family is the natural unit for the organization of the husbandman, his work should teach him the importance of his function as a procreator. It is hardly an accident that with tremendous urban growth the denial of breeding values is always present.

Those reared only on bread and circuses may claim the more unreal responsibility of a vote, but they can and do lose the tradition of trusteeship and the instinct of sound perpetuation. The instinct to choose a lifelong partner and home-maker with health and stamina, both physical and spiritual, is warped into attraction which mistakes a spurious sex appeal for true vitality, and the mutual capacity to enjoy tinsel amusements with the character to share life. They become the mob rushing to destruction. Only half-conscious that they have lost the status of life, they clamour against the truth which whispers that "the fault lies not in our stars, but in ourselves." Uncertain of themselves they both deny and hate inherent superiority.

The farmer knows full well the importance of environment, and he does not belittle it. But he knows that without sound stock and type he will not flourish. He will not willingly or wittingly sow bad seed or use bad sires. When people are in true harmony with Nature there is least often unsound mating among human beings. Men and women learn instinctively to choose a good type for each other. This is of supreme importance among ourselves in Great Britain where the Industrial Revolution has gone far to smother such sound instinct, and where the scientist and priest have been too prone to gratify the delusions of the mob with half-truths.

The results of our false values in suicidal economics has meant that the sound in every walk of life have had an increasing burden thrust upon them to support the wreckage of the system. The State has dealt meanly with its servants in Army, Navy, or Imperial Civil Services. The devoted men who brought order and justice to, and fought famine and disease in India and elsewhere have not been able to perpetuate their kind. They had to choose between serving a great purpose or bringing up a family large enough to carry on their blood. We have forgotten that taxation for social services, or repayment of the usurer must ultimately fall upon the shoulders of the primary producer. Taxation has fallen more hardly upon the responsible individual than the exploiter and speculator. Social maintenance has supported in far too many cases the incompetent at the expense of the better workman who tries to succour his family with his efforts, unaided by the State. The unwholesome and the feckless have been helped to flourish. This does not mean that we should leave the hindmost to the devil, but that our social efforts should have been based on values which should first aim at the survival of the best in mind and body.

A Ballade of Inevitable Mechanisation

by Harold Robbins

"The Machine has come to stay."

—Lord Bledisloe,[10] *the ninety-seventh and, let us hope, the last Modern Thinker to make this Interesting Discovery.*

The Norseman came to Portland Bay
And took my niece with all his crew.
I did not arm me for the fray,
A noble viscount whom I knew
Said, "Let me press this fact on you –
Your strong dislikes of rape betray
The narrow, unprogressive view,
For Norsemen's raids have come to stay."

A slinking lawyer made me pay
Because I had no deeds to view.
He stole my land, and on a day
He took possession with his shrew.
I to my trusty viscount flew
Who said to me: "Why be a jay?
'Tis thus the grand old squiredom grew:
And squiredom, it has come to stay."

I struck him then. He sent Lord Hay
To ask me for my seconds. Few
Would help me in that dread mélée:
At all events, there was no queue.
We met at dawn, and stripped and drew.
I did not wish the man to slay:
I murmured, as I ran him through,
The Duello has come to stay.

ENVOI

My Lord, you make me sick. The Zoo
May take things as they come. But pray,
Learn from our fathers how Men *do*.
Nothing we hate has come to stay.

Sydney
R Jones
1911

IV
Cottagers
by H. J. Massingham

WHY WAS THE OLDER COTTAGER SO TOUGH AND hardy? The answer is silence, for no social historian has considered the significance of such records as exist. Yet a very large proportion of our older cottagers lived to a ripe old age after a lifetime of arduous labour and in spite of such evils as fevers from insanitary conditions and rheumatism from constant exposure. A friend, for instance, tells me of a Worcestershire dame of ninety-one who ran a small farm herself and at the same time brought up a family of twelve, besides adopting five other children. She made every variety of home wines and was famed for her mushroom catsup. Ordered to dress the meadow which provided her mushrooms with chemicals during the last war, she refused, but the field was forcibly fed. It has bred no mushrooms since. Last year, I heard of a Sussex woman of 109 years 5 months, who had worked hard all her long Old Testamentish life. On the day of her death she went down to the chicken run to feed the fowls and there dropped dead. The men of Arnhem died no better.

I may append to these testimonies another one from an estate agent who gave me what is perhaps the rarest of all the exhibits in my collection of "bygones," a pigmy flail with moulded handles and used with one hand for threshing out turnip or grass seeds.

> What a thousand pities it is that we have not more of the real old farm-labourers left today! Grand men most of them were, and they were experts. Although I am

---

* *This chapter is taken from "Cottagers," Chapter 6 of* The Wisdom of the Fields *(London: Collins, 1945), pp. 106–115.*

> agent for this place and have been for years, there are few jobs on a farm that I cannot do from hand-shearing upwards and downwards, and it was those men you write of that taught me. It was not a soft school either, and I well remember going for five successive years with one of the old sheep-shearing gangs—first year, catch and tie for them; second year, catch, tie up the fleeces and open up the bellies of the sheep—after that I was promoted to the actual shearing, which I had to learn to do with both hands. We started daily at 4 a.m. till 8 a.m. and then on till noon with half an hour out. One p.m. to 4.30, then tea for half an hour and then on till 8 p.m. when we were done for the day. In five years of my time as pupil at one farm, I never had a half-day off that I did not have to make up on my day's work first. How many of the youngsters of today would stand that pressure?

Another letter came from an old-time scythe man whose ground for writing was that he could not bear the countryside to be regarded "merely as an annexe to the big cities" nor Nature to be "reduced to a matter of figures and machines."

When he was eleven and a carter's lad, he used to walk ten miles every Sunday to see his parents and ten miles back again to start milking. When he was thirteen, he milked, bedded down, and tended seven cows without any help. About 1880 he became ploughman and carter on a farm near Leek, working from 6 a.m. to 9 p.m. and as well as his normal work carrying coal from the pithead. At harvest, he also went out into the cornfields with a group of twelve or twenty using the "badging hook," and into the hay with the scythe. When he was twenty-three he got married and took on a holding of twelve acres of his own, running it with his wife as well as working as a labourer for neighbouring farmers. In off-times he used to break four tons of stone a day at the parish quarry. He cleaned "dykes" and preferred the rate of 2d. the rood of eight yards to that of 8s. a week because he could make more. Once a week, he used to walk six miles to Leek market carrying a basket with 200 eggs in it on one arm with 12 pounds of butter on the other.

Such examples could be multiplied indefinitely by research not into books but the memories of old cottagers. I shall give but one more because it concerns Harry Rogers of the last chapter. His father, Tommy, was a poacher in the picaresque tradition of the nineteenth century countryside. He drank nothing but beer (in almost fabulous quantities), never wore an overcoat and lived hale to eighty-two. "They," as Edmund Blunden[11] has written:

> They were men of pith and thew
> Whom the city never called.

I believe that one of the reasons for the robust longevity of the old folk was the survival of pride and satisfaction in work after their nurse, personal ownership, had been taken from them by the Enclosures. They in their turn depended upon the vitality of the small more or less self-supporting local community which was also long a-dying. I quote from a letter received from a Greek weaver of tapestries, carpets and brocades. It gives an oblique glimpse of the kind of independence, self-support and worthwhileness in work that drew *Cottage Economy* from Cobbett.[12]

> My father was a fruit-grower in Greece where I was brought up, and this heredity and upbringing have left their mark. I have revisited Greece many times since and it saddens me to see all the changes that have taken place, especially during the last twenty or thirty years. In my childhood, the peasant arts though declining were not yet dead, and in my father's youth every single item of food was produced on the parental farm and all the textiles and household requisites such as soap, candles, etc., were made in the home. There were no "shops" in the town but only "workshops" and articles like furniture, pottery, hardware and utensils of all kinds were ordered and bought on the site where they were made. Itinerant vendors supplemented or supplied the needs of the smaller households.

A "primitive" way of life? One at any rate highly favourable to the health and happiness of the community.

This introduces the second and allied reason for the vigour of the cottager against bad pay, bad drainage and overwork. It was the quality of the food eaten. I turn again to my correspondent, the scythe man. He lived mainly on oatmeal cakes "shaped like gramophone records." Every cottage had its own "bakston" or bake-oven for baking the oatmeal which was eaten with homemade butter or cheese. Almost the only meat was home-snared rabbit or pork and cured hams from the cottager's pig. There were wines from the home-hedges, trout and pike from the farm fishpond and a restricted amount of orchard and cottage-garden fruit. Then comes what may have been the most important item of all. "Contractors used to collect night-soil from the towns and sell it to the farmers for their land."

Food was thus organically grown. But the methods of preparing it must also be taken into account. Another letter I received was from Mrs. Peggy Goodman, who farms in Wales and is an authority on milling oatmeal. She wrote in high praise of the traditional Welsh folk-cookery as tested not only by its palatability but by the number of elderly people found in every village who had profited by it. Their sight, hearing and digestions were quite unimpaired by age, as was their physical and mental vitality. One of them was a Welshman who lived on Welsh oatmeal in hot water from the age of sixty-five onwards, one large bowlful every day. He died at 104. But it was not the same story with those younger people who had replaced the oatmeal, milk, butter and potatoes of these veterans' childhood with white bread, margarine and tea. Cobbett's belief in wholeness of living was not, therefore, theoretic. It was based on his own observations on the benefits of physical health and psychological sanity derived from it.

*****

So MUCH for the individual cottager between his time and ours. But Cobbett's appraisal of the past was based on his cottagers having formed self-supporting communities. The Enclosures, he said, had produced effects so injurious that those responsible for them "might begin to suspect that the 'dark age' people were not so very foolish when they had so many common fields and when almost every man that had a family had also a bit of land, either large or small." A letter to me from the local historian, Dr. W. G. Hoskins,[13] describes the Leicestershire village of Wigston Magna as an example of a free and self-governing cottager community. It was composed mainly of peasant proprietors without a resident lord since Doomsday "or even earlier." They made their own bye-laws for village and field, managed their own church and its finances, ran their own guild and "in short did everything for themselves and were an absolutely independent community." Their mode of life, he added, was a "civilisation in the best sense of the word."

Had Cobbett been alive today, he would still have found many smallholders, but only a minority practising subsistence husbandry and that incompletely. He would have found only one village, Laxton[14] in Nottinghamshire, where the system of common fields survived in conjunction with family holdings. He would have become aware of a strong movement in high places for the dispossession of the smallholder as "uneconomic" and the absorption of his plots in "large-scale economic units," a final instalment of the Enclosures. A letter from a smallholder who cultivates or cultivated 17 acres on the southern slopes of Dartmoor explains the consequences of the War Agricultural Committee (W.A.R.) insisting on him becoming a part-time worker off his holding and throws an oblique light on this movement:

> I told the W.A.C. I couldn't do more than I was doing here. But they were determined that the small subsistence farm must go and I must become an insured worker. They say we produce nothing: we feed 8 people almost entirely, sell several dozen eggs a week, several tons of potatoes each year, hundreds of cabbages and broccoli, sacks of sprouts, one or two yearlings, about 6 pigs for bacon (purchased at a loss). This year we had finally to say good-bye to the tractor, and we do all our own work in every respect. This year, too, we hoped for the first

> satisfactory profit, £100 in kind and £125 in cash, less £25 expenses. This country I feel is hopeless from our point of view. All we can hope is to keep our family together until we can get out. They made it clear that our way of life must go. As the W.A.C. told me, "You must move with the times or get out."

I turn to a larger farmer of a much richer piece of land. This farmer "moves with the times" so heartily that, returning nothing, he has taken since the war five white straw crops in succession. Presumably because he is so well abreast of the times, the W.A.C. has left him indulgently alone. In what direction are the times actually moving? Starvation looks Europe in the face, and there are no further areas of virgin soil in the world to be exploited for "cheap food."

Cobbett, in his Rural Ride through the twentieth century, would have come into contact with one community of smallholders at once numerous, vigorous, and prosperous. How has such a community contrived to survive and in what ways does it conform to, in what fail to conform to, the principles laid down in *Cottage Economy*? Does it fulfil the first mission of the smallholder, to provide a good living for his family from his own production and sell his surplus, preferably to the neighbours, as provision for the rainy days? Or, like the farmer above, does it sell everything off the holding in exchange for cash? Are the holdings mixed and do the wives bake and cure bacon and pursue the domestic crafts? Have they by this wholeness of living achieved something like a local and co-operative democracy like that of Wigston? If so, how can it maintain itself in the face of an economic system that aggravates the evils Cobbett saw in its earlier phases?

The example comes from the Vale of Evesham and the answer to these questions is mixed. But one answer is unequivocal. The smallholders of the Vale, living side by side with market growers of big acreages but not depressed by them, owe their flourishing condition, not to the soil as is erroneously supposed, but to a very ancient system of land tenure, the "Evesham Custom." It was created, not by the enlightenment of squire or lord of the manor, but the old Commoners themselves. The present system of tenancy is directly founded upon it. My knowledge both of the history of the Evesham smallholders and their present life and economy is derived from my own explorations of the region in the nineteen thirties and from my old friend, Mr. C. H. Gardiner, Clerk to the District Council.

Good cultivation in the Evesham region goes back as far as 700 A.D. when the monks of Evesham Abbey established not only market-gardening and fruit-growing but the smallholder. All the records of the Borough reveal that the small master thrived there for more than a thousand years under the open field system. Then came the Enclosures and down he went. But when farms became vacant in the depression after 1874, the landlords, remembering the consequences of the past, cut them up and let them to the labourers. The opportunity was given them of cultivating their new farms according to the counsels of *Cottage Economy*. They took it and became entirely self-subsistent. They used only family labour and lived on what they produced. They were heartened in this epic struggle by two signal advantages. One was the frequent presence of Joseph Arch[15] in the neighbourhood with his programme of small independent mastership. The other was the survival of the Evesham Custom of their forefathers.

This gave the small man two securities and incentives. One was a very unusually generous valuation of tenant right which enabled him to profit by intensive cultivation of and improvements to his land. The other was the power of nominating a new tenant to his landlord who, if satisfactory, was bound to be accepted. This meant that notices to quit were and are rare. The equally unusual enlightenment of the County Council and the Small Holdings and Allotments Act of 1908 had the effect of ratifying and extending the encouragements of the Custom.

Yet in the Borough the average holding per man is only 7.5 acres and the larger peasants rarely cultivate more than 20 to 40 acres. There are few landless and even the casual labourer tills a small plot. The wife shares her husband's self-respect and independence by herself earning on the land. House-pride and so the housewifely crafts of jam-making, wine and cider-making and other domestic arts are normal. The social relations between master and workman retain the old friendliness and familiarity there; reciprocal services and co-operation are a common feature of the local life. In the spring of this year (1945), for instance, thirty of these smallholders, including a soldier on leave and a boy to hand round tots of cider, turned up to put to rights the asparagus bed of one of their number who was ill. There was no committee nor overseer and the spontaneity of the neighbourly act was taken for granted in all the villages about. Fifty years ago, ten villages combined to have a piped water-supply installed, and horses are jointly owned today as oxen were in the pre-Enclosure village. Every inch of land is utilised, the marshy bits being planted with withies for tying the abundant produce. While the farming population of the Vale has declined, the small holding one has doubled itself in a century and the Parish Councils are active. Before local milling of whole-grain flour was made illegal by a Government acting thus as the agent of the milling combine, the Valesmen grew wheat for local milling. Their women baked the flour in their own ovens and set aside the bran for the cottage pig. The passages on bread and pig-keeping in *Cottage Economy* might have been texts on the homestead's wall.

The traditional background of this busy and enterprising community is thus manifest. A particular witness in point is the survival of the strip system of the open fields whereby the holdings of a villager were scattered over the whole parish, some on the good ground, some on the poor, for fairness' sake. This practice set the advocates of Enclosure in full cry: what could be more time-wasting and uneconomic than for the peasant holder to be plodding to and fro with his carts and implements between one of his strips and another, perhaps half a mile away? Why then do the virile smallholders of Evesham Vale retain the antiquated principle of the scattered strip? For three very good reasons. It enables them to live in their own villages instead of on their holdings which they easily reach by bicycle. Thus the village community remains compacted. It makes practicable the growing of particular crops in the different areas best suited to them and each holder to order his crop varieties into a pattern. Thirdly, he can increase or reduce his various strips as need or convenience arises. But the real answer is that the system works extremely well, as doubtless it did in the open fields community or it would not have survived for a thousand years.

All who know the small holdings of the Vale testify to their extraordinary productiveness. Yet the Vale soil, though good, is not exceptional. Being low-lying, it is liable to flooding from the Avon and to late May frosts. Part of it is clay land, which requires the continuous working that only the peasant or his descendant gives to it, and part the much lighter "river terrace" soils most liable to be affected by drought. Mr. Gardiner told me that a smallholder, showing a party round, remarked:

> The soil's nothing to do with it. You could dump us anywhere in England and in two years we should have adjusted ourselves to local soils and other conditions, and we'd be on our feet.

A. H. Savory in *Grain and Chaff from an English Manor* (1885) wrote of the Evesham labourers struggling to become land-holders:

> These men, by their unceasing labour and self-denial, were just beginning to turn the corner; they had cleaned the land, ameliorated its mechanical condition by application of soot and deep digging with their beloved forks . . . and the well-merited return was coming in increasingly year by year.

It is vital, therefore, to observe how these men of the spade and fork have coped with modern machinery. In my experience, the craftsman and the husbandman not only do know how to cope with it without forfeiting the personal skill of and interest in their work but are the only existing types who can. The Valesman uses a small motor cultivator which is in fact nothing more than a power-driver, breast-plough. I have one of these in my collection of agricultural bygones. A glance at it reveals its very bulkiness and unwieldiness as a measure of the high skill it once exacted. Now mechanical power has circumvented the primitiveness of the implement without sacrificing the aptitude of its use. Men of the Vale still take it to the local blacksmith for adjustments and attachments to fall in with particular needs. Man is still the master. This is of supreme importance to those who desire man to remain and continue as man. Yet for years before the war the busybodies were at the Valesmen. They were "uneconomic"; they were not scientific and technical enough, while Sir Daniel Hall[16] proposed hitching them on compulsorily to become "producing units in large-scale enterprise." Mr. Gardiner is anxious about their future. To save them from commercial and totalitarian attentions, he exhorts these traditional peasants to take a dose of "technical education and scientific research." Being what they are, they can be trusted to do so without fear of an overdose, just as they can be trusted with machinery. One of them, visiting a soil analyst at the Long Ashton Research Station,[17] mentioned that "scientific research" is useless unless subordinate to practical experience, just as automatic machinery is an incubus unless subordinate to hand-skill. It is for what they are, not for what they do, that they are imperilled. They produce abundantly without the aid of bulldozers and multiple ploughs. But it is because they are small rural peasants that they are out of favour.

V
The Agricultural Village
by H. Robbins

YOU ARE, PROBABLY, THE NORMAL SORT OF HUMAN being in whom an idea evokes an image. Being this normal sort of person, if you think of England–not the England of which most of us have cause to be ashamed–but the England you are overworking, or fighting, or dying to preserve and recreate: then the image which will arise first in your mind is almost certainly the image of an English village.

For the village is the very genius of England, and this is not rhetoric but sober truth. It stands for England not only in the mind of the villager, but in the mind of the fighting industrial townsman as he longs for home: even the Cockney[18] has this concept. For no one familiar with *working* London can be unaware of the exciting paradox that by very reaction from its hugeness London has taken on many of the attributes of a congeries of villages. (This by the way.)

The village is not planned, but it follows always a plan emerging from the ultimate reality it serves. Its houses are partly from the full flood of the tradition–these are mostly past their best–and partly from an age which was invariably deplorable in its building. It is the considerable achievement of the village to have digested all but the worst of these. It has a few larger dwellings on its outskirts, which will be a proof that even the Tudor and Stuart millionaires could not achieve ugliness. Its inn has a temperature well above that of the brewery company which has tried to impose its frigid urban efficiency.

* *This chapter is taken from "The Agricultural Village,"* The Cross and the Plough, *Ss. Peter and Paul, 1947, pp. 10–12.*

Its village hall is probably the village eyesore–proof of a living spirit which lacked its ancient means. Its church is certainly the loveliest thing in it. (I apologise to my unknown colleague for mentioning the Church. It is a comfort to reflect that writing his own article he is probably unable to refrain from mentioning the land.) But the Church. It is probably the key to our problem, and has evoked the same image a hundred times, that what is broad-based upon the living earth must point to heaven if it is to keep its soul.

No architect designed this village. No architect has ever equalled the achievement of its humble builders. For the village is an effect and not a cause. It is organic and functional–living and having its being in the life of the land.

This must be our explanation of survival and our key to the future. The village, battered, starved and abused, has survived because it is essential to the only thing stronger than industrialism. Nothing in the Scott Report was so admirable as its appreciation and insistence that the English landscape, including the English village, is a consequence of the work of the English on the land, and that it cannot be preserved or recreated if that work suffers radical change.

Many testimonies converge. Mr. Peter Drucker,[19] that strong thinker, has written recently *The Future of Industrial Man*. Significantly, it is chiefly about the past of non-industrial man. He lays down the undoubted truth that the modern strains and disintegration arise from the fact that "Western society is still fundamentally pre-industrial in its social beliefs and values"–whereas "decisive power is derived from no one but the managers themselves, controlled by nobody and responsible to no one."

Pre-industrial beliefs and values created the village. It follows that they must survive and flourish for the village to survive and flourish.

We arrive at this starting point for the future, only to realise with a shock that most of our Planners are trying to revive the villages by giving them as many urban (and worse, suburban) values as possible. One would have thought that the achievements of industrialism, at all events for the village, would have been a warning rather than an example. For if, as we must assume, the function of the village is to make villagers happy, the standards of happiness achieved in industrial towns by industrial means are—to use a remarkable understatement—at least irrelevant.

Our Planners, however, have ordered the attendant goblins to provide "*a bumper of the same, for Mr. Grub.*"

Let us keep to the point. An English village is the result, not the cause, of a way of life and a habit of mind. If we want such villages, we must revive that way and habit.

It was the chief mark of the men who built the villages that they were yeomen owning, or at least controlling effectively, land in small units with a high degree of self-sufficiency. If we are to restore anything like what we understand by a village, farms must tend to become not larger but smaller, not specialised but mixed, not mechanised but rich in animal husbandry.

It does not matter whether you like this prospect or not. If you want villages you must have this basis for them. Only so will you revive the rich local life—the blacksmith, wheelwright, saddler and carpenter as well as the farmer—all contributing their characteristic quota to the community soul which produced this supreme thing.

Now, free and prosperous men on and about the land will certainly improve the villages. Free and prosperous men always cherish the good estate of their women-folk and children.

But it does not follow that they will want to do it in a way characteristic (and no doubt necessary) in large towns. They will certainly want good water, for example. But it is by no means certain that they will want it piped from a dozen miles away, and perhaps not piped at all. Wells are congenial to the rural condition. All we have forgotten is that they need, not only sinking, but cleaning. Here is another rural craft which flourished once and has gone with the rural decay. Nor do I think it certain that a free village would choose to be lighted by an electric supply whose pylons affront the day.

They might even decide that Hollywood and Elstree[20] films have no appeal for them. And they might decide that many special pleasures depend on the building of a village hall comparable in loveliness and dignity to the village church.

In the Middle Ages, of course, the nave of the church was thought suitable for many village functions which would shock us in such a site today. Well and good. They will in that case tear down the hideous wooden hut which was all their poverty afforded, and erect a seemly place, probably next to the Inn.

I do not know. No one can be sure until we have the free men in their little holdings. All I am insisting on here is that we are starting at the wrong end if we begin by reconstructing villages as much on the lines of the nearest large town as possible.

We are back to origins.

Let us begin with the first things. Let us not, as a wise old friend said to me recently, in our anxiety to remove the physical stress from life, replace it with a psychological stress which will complete the ruin, among other ruins, of the English village.

Two practical dangers clamour for remedy.

The great town has damned itself. It is proposed to disperse industry into the countrysides. I express no opinion on the propriety of that course so far as small towns are concerned. That is not my function here. But unless industry can be decentralised to a point where it could take on again, and take happily, the quality of craftsmanship, it would be a disaster to extend industry to the village. It simply will not fit into that social unit as we know and value it. Not only would it affront the countrymen who through a century of inconceivable economic oppression and cultural hardships, have kept the villages alive. It would complete the destruction of the village spirit.

The other danger is complementary. The huge mechanised farms which are being advocated in many furtive quarters would destroy irrevocably that rich and diverse life of the village which depends for its validity on the intimate interplay of many strong characters formed by strong crafts. The best we could expect under such a system would be a succession of rural Bournvilles; and the most sympathetic member of the Cadbury[21] family would hardly claim that Bournville was recognisable as a village.

At worst, we might be faced with the squalor of the huge monocultural estates of the Southern United States, or an arable wilderness hideous with the gyrotiller by day and abandoned with the time siren for the nearest town by night. (It is, of course, quite untrue that mechanised agriculture produces more food per acre. The contrary is true. Small units produce more per acre. The large produce less with fewer men.)

We can have any sort of government we deserve. We cannot have any type of economic layout we desire, for the material order is conditioned by the natural asset. We have forgotten two things of decisive importance. Industrialised methods have so eroded and exhausted the soils of the world that the period of easy food from the ends of the earth has gone forever.

And industrialism has invaded so wantonly the world's stocks of irreplaceable raw materials that the period of imposed retrenchment is well in sight.

Add to these two enormous facts that, as Mr. Walter Elliot[22] reminded us recently in *The Times*, we must be prepared for Africa, Asia and Russia to industrialize on the scale of sixty per cent of their populations.

It follows that the future of England is on the land. It follows that the accumulated soil fertility which we owe to the prudence of our ancestors is now England's capital asset. It follows that we must remember peasantries have always been conservators of soil fertility; and *latifundia*, everywhere and always, exhaustive of it.

And it follows that if we wish our Commonwealth indeed to last for a thousand years, we also must clear our minds of cant. We must see things stark, scrap the prejudices and fashions of a lifetime, and bring into being that race of small English farmers which alone can act in conformity with the conditions imposed upon us. If we do this, we shall achieve our finest hour. Certainly we shall bequeath intact to the future the good England seen from the Village Green.

VI
Man's Conquest of Nature
by K. L. Kenrick

THE DEAN OF ST. PAUL'S[23] AND PROFESSOR A.D. Ritchie,[24] reviewing Bertrand Russell's[25] recent *History of Western Philosophy*, both call attention to the following passage:

> Man, formerly too humble, begins to think of himself almost as a God. In all this I feel a grave danger, the danger of what may be called cosmic impiety. The concept of "truth" as something dependent on facts largely outside human control has been one of the ways in which philosophy has hitherto inculcated the necessity of humility. When this check on pride is removed a further step is taken on the road to a certain kind of madness, to which modern men are prone. I am persuaded that this intoxication is the greatest danger of our time, and that any philosophy which contributes to it is increasing the danger of vast social disaster.

The way of the unbeliever is hard, and his difficulties are many and great. All this is admirably exemplified in the foregoing passage. The sceptic can hardly put pen to paper without proclaiming the urgent importance of those things whose very existence he is always trying to deny. He is like the enemy of formal logic and metaphysics who wants to say that every statement ever made is false, but cannot do so because he would have to include his own statement in the general holocaust. So here the phrase "cosmic impiety" is the phrase of a man who wants to deny the existence of God but cannot do so because

* *This chapter is taken from "Man's Conquest of Nature,"* The Cross and the Plough, *Ladyday, 1947, pp. 16–18.*

he feels the breath of the Hound of Heaven hot on the back of his neck. Outside the philosophy of the Christian faith there is confessedly no cosmos, only the infinite potentialities of chaos. If there is no cosmos, there is nothing to be pious about; there can be no cosmic piety, and therefore no cosmic impiety. Otherwise we are bound to say that cosmic impiety is as essential a feature of the process as is cosmic piety.

The instant we begin to admit the idea of a cosmos, we are on the road to Rome; we are almost within earshot of the accents of the Holy Father. Theologians have known for two thousand years that there was a vast social disaster awaiting mankind. When it involves the innocent with the guilty, they call it "the wrath of God"; when it meticulously discriminates between innocent and guilty, they call it "Hell." They have also known that the way to Hell was through the sin of pride, and that what could save man from it was the virtue and grace of humility. But there is nothing in the whole of Mr. Russell's philosophy to warrant any such deduction, or to justify either of these two statements. There is no room in it for sin or virtue or grace.

A friend of mine calls logic the democratic science that defends the common man against the tyranny of the expert. The expert must have his million-pound laboratory, but the student of logic does not even need a book. Mr. Russell is one of the experts; as logicians we may legitimately ask him what authority he has for saying that man has ever been too humble, and who gave him that authority. He speaks of the "necessity of humility." Who would complain of a sphere as being too spherical, or of a picture as being too beautiful, or of a piece of music as being too musical? Is the whole of his philosophy based on foundations no less flimsy?

And why should Mr. Russell trouble himself and his readers about the possibility of vast social disaster? If the human race is merely a plague of vermin on the fair face of the earth, and if each one of us is no better than a rat, why worry? What does it matter what happens to us? There is nothing axiomatically important about the future of the race, and the democratic logician is bound to ask for an adequate reason for the concern demanded of him. The instant we admit that man is something better than a rat, we are once more on the road to Rome. Before we know where we are we shall be talking about man having an immortal soul. What conceivable difference can there be between man and rat if both are destined to the same doom? The geologists talk of a race of pre-historic monsters which were suddenly involved in some cataclysmic disaster and disappeared. Who now worries about their end? They were a magnificent race, in many ways more magnificent than puny man, but who cares? I am constantly being told, by all sorts of experts, to exercise all sorts of precautions about my physical welfare. But if I take no thought for my immortal soul, why should I take thought for my mortal body? What is there about my body that makes it so much more important than my soul? Frankly, I can see nothing in my body that makes it worth preserving for five minutes.

There are spots on the sun. When we in these columns have pointed out all the fallacies we can find in Mr. Russell's statement, we are bound to admit that we recognise in it a statement of the greatest value and of the utmost importance. His words are the words of a wise man, who, in spite of the most strenuous efforts, has failed to break away from the great Christian tradition in which he has been brought up. He here gives utterance to a great Catholic truth. He rejects the Christian faith root and branch, but he must have its flowers and fruit because he cannot live without them. Who has once seen the Cross, however imperfectly and inadequately, can never again be as though he had never seen it. So Bertrand Russell here cuts himself off from his own philosophy and says what Christian men have said throughout the ages. Indeed, when a Catholic priest says exactly the same thing, we Catholics always say, "How dull! how commonplace! how conventional! how uninspired and uninspiring!" although we know it is perfectly true.

The price of liberty is eternal vigilance. Many think that the danger is from the extreme left, others think it is from the extreme right. To us in these columns the words "left" and "right" mean next to nothing. If we thought it worthwhile we would insist on adequate definitions in significant language, but it is not worthwhile. For one thing, we realize that to a certain extent we are bound to submit to the current terminology, but more important still, we have perfect confidence in the thousands of excellent fellows who are on the watch for the dangers from extreme left and extreme right. To employ the same foolish nomenclature, our concern is with the danger from the extreme centre. We believe that the greatest danger comes from the most unexpected quarter, the point where everything looks perfectly safe and where no-one has ever thought of setting a watch. This is where we want the best men to be, and this is where we claim Bertrand Russell as a valuable ally. When we see left and right glaring at each other across the floor, we feel comparatively safe and comfortable. We think there is a possibility that they will keep each other in check to some extent. When thieves fall out, honest men may come by their own. But when we see left and right making for the centre, when we see them begin to smile genially at each other and shake hands with each other and congratulate each other on each other's speeches, then we begin to think it is time to feel apprehensions and misgivings. Bertrand Russell is generally set down as something of a Communist, but here at least he rises above all the ideologies and talks about a danger which is at its greatest when the ideologists have forgotten all their differences. It is when both sides begin to say the same things, in the same words and in the same tone of voice, about "Man's Conquest of Nature," "the Importance of Economic Interdependence," "the Industrialisation of Agriculture," "the Future of Atomic Energy," "the Leisure State," *that* is when and where "cosmic impiety" begins; that is when and where man "begins to think of himself as a God"; that is when and where man begins to forget "the necessity of humility." To what other kind of thing but this can Bertrand Russell be referring? I can think of nothing else. All these phrases represent aspects of a vast comprehensive philosophy which is taking possession of all men and making them forget their littleness, their insignificance, their extreme dependence. They are the phrases of intoxicated men and madmen who think of themselves, not as creatures, but as creators. If Bertrand Russell is not generalising in the void (and that I cannot believe of him), this must be what he is aiming at. What alternative suggests itself?

Of all these proud phrases, perhaps the proudest and maddest is the one about "Man's conquest of nature." If Bertrand Russell is right, we must not only abstain from propagating philosophies which minister to men's pride, but must fight these philosophies, in all their aspects, whenever and wherever they raise their ugly heads. Is man really conquering nature, or is nature conquering man? When I was a boy, I had as much butter to eat as I liked. At the present moment, I feel doubtful whether I shall ever taste butter again. Is this because I am conquering nature, or because nature is conquering me? If we are having to send to the Antarctic for our food; if we are having to go deeper and deeper for our fuel; if we are finding it more and more difficult to recruit men for the heavy industries, on which so much is said to depend; if the birth-rate among the most highly civilised peoples is steadily declining; if we are all at the mercy of atomic energy; is it because we are conquering nature, or because nature is conquering us? And *respice finem*.[26] Are we finally to triumph over nature and live for ever, or are we all doomed to die?

The modern scientific politician who lusts to rule all men talks as if man's conquest of nature were something achieved but yesterday. Two thousand five hundred years ago Sophocles,[27] in a chorus in the *Antigone*, described the same victory far more convincingly and far more grandly than any modern expert could ever hope to do. But with Sophocles, this paean of triumph was but a prelude to the most horrifying crimes and disasters, and the last words of the chorus in the tragedy are "Great words of prideful men are ever punished with great blows, and in old age teach the chastened to be wise." Henceforth we are free to say that men who try to persuade us that a glowing future awaits mankind because we have conquered nature, are either miscreants who have their own axes to grind, or are the poor deluded victims of such miscreants. In whatever direction we look, there is no glowing future awaiting mankind. If we are allowed to live, this is as much as we can expect, and in this we must learn to find our happiness. This is the teaching of Bertrand Russell and of Sophocles, and this is the teaching of the Catholic Church.

VII
The Clergy and the Carpenter–Not Walking Hand in Hand

by Philip Hagreen

IT IS THE NATURE AND DUTY OF MAN TO WORK. He who does not work is disobeying God's law and is a parasite on other men. In spite of the Fall, and the long decline from Paradise to Pimlico,[28] there are few men who do not want to work, in one way or another.

Of this essential activity of man the clergy say little. Perhaps this is as well, for when, about once a year, they preach on the hidden life of Our Lord and speak of His work as a carpenter, what they say is usually bosh.

This excuse may be made for the clergy: that their work as priests has not changed since the time of Our Lord. Their raw material, the human soul, remains the same. Their tools are still the liturgy, the sacraments and teaching. The clergy do not realise their unique immunity from the disaster that has crippled the lives of other men. To follow the example of Our Lord as priest is still possible. To follow the example of Our Lord as carpenter is forbidden.

We are told from the pulpit that by working as a carpenter Our Lord set us an example of humility and patience: that He chose a laborious trade and endured its drudgery. We hear of a menial occupation in a provincial village and of the tedium of knocking in nils.

That He who made the oak tree by His word should therefrom have made a table by the labour of His hands was indeed

---

* *This chapter is taken from "The Clergy and the Carpenter: Not Walking Hand in Hand,"* The Cross and the Plough, *Michaelmas, 1945, pp. 6–10.*

an example of humility and patience. We would suggest that it was also an example of how tables should be made.

Let us think for ourselves what manner of work may have been done in the carpenter's shop in Nazareth. We shall find that the things made there had a reasonable purpose and that conditions favoured the right making of them. In other words, the things were works of art. They could only fail to be perfect works of art through the imperfection of the carpenter. The things made by Our Lord were therefore perfect works of art: the only perfect works of art that the world has seen.

There are moot points about St. Joseph's work. What, for instance, was the range of it? Did it include what we should now call wheelwright's work and cooper's work? Were the things made mostly agricultural gear such as ploughs, harrows, and ox-yokes; or household furniture and utensils? Was the carpenter's shop also a smithy, and, if so, were nails, hinges, etc., made of iron or bronze? Of other points, and these the essentials of right making, we can be certain.

Firstly, the things made were for reasonable and good purposes. They supplied the normal needs of the neighbourhood. St. Joseph dealt directly with his customers, who could discuss their requirements with him. If he were asked to make a bad thing he could refuse. In other words, the *final cause* of each thing was good and was clearly known to its maker.

Secondly, the raw material, the wood, was local. Trees were felled by St. Joseph, or under his supervision, and their barking, cleaving and stacking were his concern. It is not the nature of most trees to have much straight grain, and it is not the nature of woodwork to have only plane surfaces. A straight-grained piece may be set aside for a table-top, while pieces of suitable curve are selected for ploughs, etc. The saw was mainly used across the grain, where it cuts sweetly. Along the grain, the tree was opened with wedges. This is a delightful process, leaving the full strength of the wood and revealing its full beauty. Such wood will not warp, and for many purposes it may be used at once and allowed to season at its leisure. St.

Joseph was free to choose the most suitable wood for each part of a job. Thus the *material cause* of the work was good.

Thirdly, St. Joseph's bench and tools were his own, probably because he had made them. He was free to replace them or alter and adapt them to his needs. They fitted their user, being of the right weight and proportions for his stature and strength. Thus the *efficient cause* of the work was good.

Fourthly, there remains the *formal cause*, the practical intelligence of the carpenter. In St. Joseph's case this was certainly good. In Our Lord's case it was perfect.

When a Jesuit tells us that Our Lord chose the dull work of a common carpenter rather than the more interesting work of a cabinet maker, the poor man is talking through his biretta. It is hard nowadays to make anyone understand what was meant by craftsmanship, because so few have ever seen any. The only skill people can appreciate now is in games. Well then, the specialised precision of the cabinet-maker may be likened to billiard-playing. The all-round woodworker, swinging axe or adze, slicing with the draw-knife and dealing with incalculable curves, may be likened rather to the cricketer, who must be able to bowl and bat and catch and run. His work depends on decisions in the air, on movements too subtle for measurement and too swift for conscious calculation. It shows a right instinct in the average Englishman that he respects the billiard champion but that he feels something of hero-worship towards the great cricketer.

A learned priest tells us that the curse of Adam seems to have worked itself out, since machinery has removed the drudgery from work. We wonder how the clergy would like it if *their* work were mechanised, modernised, rationalised. If the sub-division of labour allotted to each priest not even one recognisable word of the Mass but only one meaningless syllable which he was compelled to repeat, as fast as he could stutter it, all day long and all the year round. Perhaps some of them would only jib at the long hours, for their Mass sounds very much like that as things are.

If a carpenter does bad work, the clergy think it no libel to say that he is a bad carpenter. Yet if we speak of a bad priest they think we are accusing him of unchastity, for it does not occur to them that a bad priest might be one who does a priest's work badly.

The words used about making are worthy of meditation. For instance, we admit the merit of a thing that is *hand-made.* But the hand is used in mechanised production. The hand is all that is used. We therefore call such production manufacture and speak of the employees as hands. The merit of the hand-made thing is that it is made by *man.* The craftsman uses his memories of tradition and of experience. He uses his understanding to apply these to the job in hand, and he uses his will to do the job as well as he can in the best way he can think of. Thus his hand is directed by the three powers of his soul and the thing is made by the whole man. So naturally do we think of the hand as the executive of the soul that we speak of acts of the Divine Will as the work of God's hand. Note that a steam-ship carries so many hands. A sailing-ship carried so many souls.

All that exists is made by God, directly or indirectly. The daisy praises God because it is as He made it. It lives and grows and multiplies and withers in perfect conformity to His will. The bird, acting by the instinct that God gives it, builds a nest. That nest is part of God's creation and He sees that it is good. The carpenter makes a table, but the carpenter is prone to evil. He may work carelessly through sloth. He may work too hastily through avarice. He may be too meticulous through pride of craftsmanship and through being wrongly ashamed of his human limitations. He may try to give his work a perfection that only belongs to things made directly by God. A cruder kind of pride may lead him to make the table, not the best way, but in a way that will show his skill or his originality.

By the virtue of art, these temptations are avoided. The carpenter may make a table to the best of his ability. It will be a perfect table: not perfect in the sense in which a daisy is perfect, but perfect in its suitability, its appropriateness. Compared with a daisy, the best table is a clumsy botch, for human skill is infinitely below that of its Creator. Yet the table is good through the good will of its maker, through the right use of his faculties. It takes its place without disharmony in God's world, and because it is a product of man's free will, the table is more pleasing to God than all the daisies that ever bloomed.

We have no fear of misrepresenting the views of the clergy on work. We have discussed the matter with so many priests in the course of so many years that we know their teaching by heart. Further, we have read many Pastoral Letters. In particular, we remember a joint pastoral of our hierarchy on the social question. Therein our bishops talked of the dignity of man. This dignity, they said, demands that he should have security of employment, a family wage, a bathroom, and suitable sanitation. They say: "As Christians we ought not to tolerate any attack, direct or indirect, on the dignity of man or on the sanctity of family life."

Very well then. We say that the dignity of man is attacked, nay, outraged, when he is compelled to spend his whole working life in sub-human, mechanical acts. We say that the sanctity of family life is violated when the husband is kept from home, virtually in prison, all his working days. When he cannot own either his means of livelihood or his home. When his children are taken from him by strangers. Of these things our spiritual leaders say not one word.

Apart from the very few priests who see that the industrial system is evil in its origins and in its effects and that no adjustment of it can make it compatible with Catholicism, the clergy are of two types.

The majority shirk the problem. They say that it is a matter of economics. That it would be too costly to make things by hand nowadays. That it would lower the standard of living. That we are not going to write with quill pens when we can have typewriters, and that, anyhow, the Church has never condemned slavery.

The other, less common, type admits the evil of industrialism, but advocates surrender to it—for the glory of God and the salvation of souls. This class includes men of learning and renown whose reputation, as well as the speciousness of their arguments, gives them great influence. It was bad when the Scribes and Pharisees were hypocrites. It is a deal worse when they are sincere.

Though these clergy admit that there are many evils connected with industrialism, they defend machinery as though its goodness were the central dogma of their faith. It would be easier to argue with them if we could discover their motive. At any mention of the evils of mechanisation, they interrupt with: "But you cannot say that machinery is evil in itself." Why are they thus roused? If a man is drowning, do they shout: "But you cannot say that water is evil in itself," or do they try to save him?

These clergy say that our idea of work is a false one. They tell us that Our Lord did not come on earth to enjoy making good woodwork but to suffer and to teach us to suffer. They say that Our Lord showed us something infinitely higher than craftsmanship, when His hands no longer held chisel and mallet but were nailed to the cross. Industrialism, they say, offers wonderful opportunities for mortifying our instincts. The acceptance of the tedium of its methods and the ugliness of its products may be means of sanctification, and this is what the workers should be taught.

Truly, every man has his cross—but woe to that man by whom he is betrayed.

These clergy say that if the work is mechanical, so much the better, as it leaves the mind free for higher things.

Mechanical work permits no use of the intellect or the will, for the actions are dictated and timed by the machine. But neither does it permit freedom of the mind. It exacts continuous attention. The punishment for a moment's inattention, hesitation or delay may be the loss of a finger or an eye, or a smash-up of machinery and an accusation of sabotage. It is only because they can give this attention that human beings are used. Whatever can be done automatically is done by machines.

In their effort to belittle the evils of industrialism, the clergy remind us that man is soul and body and that it is the soul that matters. They speak of the soul as the rider of an unruly horse and they seem to think that if the horse is lamed it will be better for the rider. But man is not two things, like rider and horse: he is soul-body, a centaur. The doctrine of the Incarnation and of the Resurrection teach us that in this life and in eternity man is one thing, a being which God has created and into which he had breathed the breath of life.

Man is not like a knife–a steel blade set in a bone handle. He is a compound like water. Water can be temporarily separated by electrolysis into oxygen and hydrogen. So can man be temporarily separated by electrocution into soul and body.

Now if we consider the duties of man on earth and his state in eternity, we must think of him as a compound, just as we must think of water as a compound when we are studying hydraulics. Oxygen and hydrogen are no concern of the hydraulic engineer. His science depends on the incompressibility of water. It is irrelevant to him that oxygen and hydrogen are compressible.

The state of man's separated soul is a mystery, for it is an incomplete substance. This is of interest to speculative theologians. The state of man's separated body is of interest to worms.

We are told that it is not economical to make things by hand. Well, let us consider the economy of such a workshop as St. Joseph's. Nothing of the material was wasted. The crooked and knotty parts of a tree were as valuable for some purposes as the straight-grained parts were for others. The bark was used by the tanner. Then it was litter and then manure. Twigs and any rotten wood were used as fuel, along with all the chips and shavings. The ash was used for washing and for the garden.

No time or energy was wasted. The carpenter could order his work to suit the rhythm of his vitality. On a frosty morning he might swing axe or adze or cleave a log with beetle and wedge. On a sultry afternoon he might sit to use the draw-knife or sharpen a saw. He could think out his problems when his mind was alert, and when it was dull he could go on with jobs that are done largely by habit. He could work in his garden when the garden needed it, or when he needed a change.

Further, no ability was wasted. There was no limit to the development of the carpenter's powers. A wooden spoon made by a man of genius surpasses ordinary spoons as a Stradivarius surpasses ordinary violins.

And what of the customer? He got what he wanted and paid only for what he got. He got a yoke that suited his breed of oxen, a harrow that suited his soil and a chair that suited his figure. The things were made to fill his needs and able to suit his means. A piece of furniture might be the cheapest that would function or it might be a highly-wrought heirloom–a joy for centuries. Most hand-made things may be repaired by their maker. They may come back to him again and again as wear or accident make it necessary. Thus he learns their weak places and devises improvements. An important point in the economy of such neighbourly dealings is that payment may often be made in kind.

Now how does this compare with the industrial methods that we are told are economical? The tree grows in some far country, perhaps on the other side of the world. Only what can be sawn into straight planks is shipped. Curved pieces would take up too much room. Instead of being seasoned and cloven, the wood is cut regardless of anything but the number of cubic feet that can be sold. Such wood is unfit for any decent work. The grain has not been followed and it will warp indefinitely. The carpenter receives it with all its best qualities destroyed. It may be full of sap or it may have been artificially seasoned–processed–so that it is as weak and characterless as cardboard. Thus the material is wasted and there is all the waste of transport by sea and land. When the wretched wood reaches the workshop or factory the carpenter may not use his wits to make the best of it. He must work to tracings made in architects' offices. Fads and fancies, or travesties of antique manners, are expressed in such terms of solid geometry as can be drawn with T-square, etc.

Thus is the *man* wasted. A man is said to be employed in the saw-mill, in the transport trade, in the design office or in the factory. Yet nowhere is the *man* employed. What is employed is the economic pressure that forces the man to perform sub-human work.

Now that finance reaps interest not only from factory production but from every kind of trade and traffic, the worker has acquired a certain value as a consumer. He has purchasing power. His wages can be sucked in again by the creators of credit. He is encouraged to raise his standard of living, which means his expenditure on rent and luxuries. It is made almost impossible for him to bring up a family or acquire permanent property. By every means he is induced to waste his wages on perishable goods, on mechanical amusement and on prefabricated emotion.

Why is such a system said to be economical? Because it pays dividends to investment, because it pays interest to credit. It is essential to mechanised industrialism that as few as possible should be employed and that their tasks should be, as far as possible, fool-proof. It is said that the workers should be contented–which means that they should be submissive. A business is considered economical if it makes profits. Its object and its test is the prosperity of parasites. If this is economy–to hell with it!

No craftsman today has the fullness of control and freedom of method that existed in St. Joseph's shop. The carpenter who starts with squared wood and machine-made nails has been robbed of three-quarters of his craft. No one today knows the joy of joining wood that he has shaped from the tree with nails that he has forged. To drive and clinch those nails gave a satisfaction that we cannot experience. The memory of it remains in our language, for the rhetorician still hits the nail on the head and clinches an argument.

There was a time in the Middle Ages when the use of glue in a joint was forbidden because the need for glue proved that a joint had not been rightly made. Now we have men classified as cabinet-makers who cannot make a dove-tail joint. Their job is to glue joints that have been cut out by machinery.

Thus has the carpenter become degraded. But how many can now spend their lives in even the most debased forms of woodwork? Very few, because wood has been ousted by materials that can be shaped entirely by machinery. Metals and plastics can be stamped and moulded without human skill. The many parts of an elaborate thing can each be mass-produced and they can be assembled by a row of slaves, each of whom repeats mechanically an allotted action. Behind him, or her, hover the "motion study expert" and the "industrial psychologist" to check any movement that is not the shortest. The production belt is speeded up to the breaking-point of human nerves. Shattering vibration, maddening noise and nauseating smells often add to the strain of the merciless speed. Hysteria may lead to the missing of a movement or even to sabotage, so those who are going crazy are discharged as unsuitable, or as suffering from "occupational neurosis," and are replaced from the great reservoir called Labour.

Industrial employment is not work, but privation. It is the crucifixion of man's nature as maker. Those who betray him to it show their love for him in the kiss of Judas. Seeing Christ in our neighbour we see him unjustly condemned. Like Pilate, we seek to release him. Most of the clergy–also like Pilate–wash their hands of the business. But the chief priests persuade the people and they cry out: "Let him be crucified!"

Illustrations

ABOVE. Gerard Wallop, the Viscount Lymington.
RIGHT. Jorian Jenks.
BELOW. A sketch of H. D. C. Pepler by his wife, Clare.

ABOVE. An engraving by Edgar Holloway (about whom see p. 12).
RIGHT. A woodcut by Hagreen advertising Robbins's 1938 book, which Dorothy Day said "contains the best thinking ever done on Distributism."
BELOW. The Peplers in front of their home, Fragbarrow House, off of Ditchling Common, Sussex, England, ca. 1918: Stephen (later Fr. Conrad), David, Margaret, H. D. C., Clare, and Nora (Clare's sister), with Janet, Mark, and Susan in the front row.

ABOVE. The crossroads on Ditchling Common, with Eric Gill's Spoil Bank Crucifix visible in the distance (see the upper left corner of the photograph).

LEFT. A postcard signed by Dorothy Sayers in 1942, bearing her portrait in charcoal sketch.

BELOW. The "Hand & Cross" by Eric Gill, engraved in 1920 as the badge of the Guild of Ss. Joseph and St. Dominic, which had its liturgical and handicraft life in the chapel and workshops in Ditchling.

ABOVE AND BELOW RIGHT. Advertisements for the Irish stout in which Dorothy Sayers combined her talents with those of John M. Gilroy (1898–1985). Gilroy was an in-house artist with S.H. Benson, Ltd., when the firm acquired the Guinness account in 1928. Sayers was a copyrighter with the firm from 1922 to 1929, and penned the poem accompanying the toucan. She also often provided the "rough scribbles" that inspired some of Gilroy's finished designs—of which there were almost 150 appearing on posters, press ads, show cards, and waiter trays from the 1930s to the '60s. Sayers also collaborated with Gilroy on the "Mustard Club" campaign for Coleman's of Norwich.

BELOW LEFT. The house of Dorothy Sayers at Witham, Essex, in England.

Above. An illustration to H.J. Massingham's *The English Countryman*, published in London in 1942. The sketch is of "An Anglo-Saxon homestead reconstructed by Marjorie and C.H.B. Quennell," included in the chapter entitled "The Old Village Economy," where Massingham writes that "there is no doubt whatever that the peasantry of our open-field system [see p. 122, n. 14] did actually achieve and live an extremely durable and tenacious peace betwen Socialism and Individualism. The community gave its adhesion to neither because it represented a fusion of them both. In it ownership and co-operation made a match of it."

Left. H.J. Massingham, his wife Penelope, and Friday, the dog.

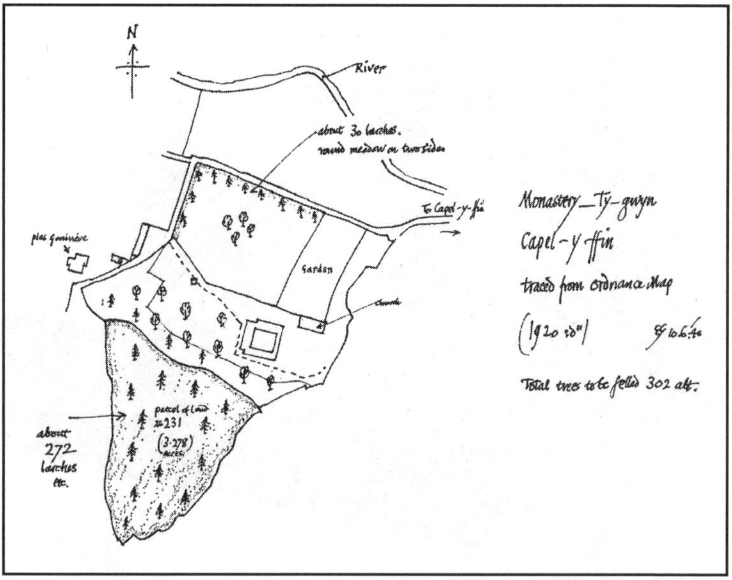

ABOVE. A map of the Monastery of Capel-v-ffyn in Wales, where Eric Gill settled with his family in 1924, drawn by Gill in 1940.

RIGHT. A fundraising appeal for the Spoil Bank crucifix, printed in Vol. III, No. 2, of the Gill-Pepler journal *The Game* in 1919.

BELOW LEFT. A self-portrait engraving by Eric Gill, 1927.

AN APPEAL

Help is wanted to put up a Crucifix on the Spoil Bank, Ditchling Common, Sussex. Money has been given or promised by soldiers as a thank-offering for their safe return from the war. It is proposed to carve on the base of the Crucifix the names of all Catholic Sailors and Soldiers from the county of Sussex who gave their lives in the war.

Subscriptions should be made payable to The Spoil Bank Fund; cheques should be crossed Barclay & Co., Burgess Hill, and sent to The Trustees, S. Dominic's Press, Ditchling, Sussex.

VIII
What of the Dustman?
by George Maxwell

APROPOS THE DIGNITY OF LABOUR. WHAT OF THE dustman? Is his labour degrading? The number of times this question is asked seems to indicate some doubt in the minds of the questioners as to whether the modern dustman's job is in accord with the right ordering of things. Not the sort of job one would choose for oneself or one's son. Not the sort of job likely to bring out the best in a man.

In order to remove doubt and arrive at a satisfactory conclusion, justice demands that the subject be examined in all its aspects and in its highest aspects first. It is to be remembered that the consideration of exceptional or abnormal circumstances does not permit of a normal conclusion to be arrived at. Where these operate the only sane procedure is so to work as to restore the normal.

The work of a dustman is to collect and dispose of dirt, filth and rubbish. Since the Fall at any rate work of this kind has been an essential factor in life, so that the question at issue would seem to be–Is it degrading for a man to be continually engaged in this occupation day in day out as is say, a priest, publican or plumber in his work?

In the highest and most noble aspect of this work we have, fortunately, the example of an institution with a charter nearly 2,000 years old, with special qualifications for dealing with the job, which has given much care and attention to the removing and disposing of dirt and filth from the souls of

---

* *This chapter is taken from "What of the Dustman?,"* The Cross and the Plough, *Michaelmas, 1944, pp. 12–13.*

men. Its labourers are highly trained in all that befits their calling. Special gifts are given to them that they carry out their work as becomes its great dignity and privilege. Universal respect is their portion for the manner in which they have carried out their work. Work which has on occasion called for the sacrifice of life, which sacrifice has been made rather than the integrity of the work be violated. It is impossible to think, apart from ignorance or perversity, that such work can be degrading. But it is of great importance here to note that essential and of every-day necessity as this work is, it has never been regarded as, or divorced from, the main work of its craftsmen and made a full-time occupation. Incidental and ancillary to his main work, it is a means to his end. The removing of that which impedes his progress in his main work. The work of making a 100% organic wholeness of life. Multiple, diverse and onerous as are the activities which this demands, there does not appear to be any desire on the part of the labourers in this sphere, for the work of spiritual dirt removal, noble as it is, to be made a full-time occupation. Why is this? On the answer to this question depends the whole issue, not only in this particular sphere but also in the lower spheres. Is there some good reason why this institution as well as its labourers fail to see the necessity for a change in their methods? Does not the vast increase in population, changed mode of life, the concentration of great masses of people in small areas and the greater accumulation of dirt and filth which these things almost inevitably entail, call for the more up-to-date economic outlook? Concentration and specialisation would facilitate the work by economising time and labour. The workman, free to give his whole attention to the work, would soon become so expert as to be able to expedite output in the most efficient manner; his mind unburdened by other considerations would digest the technical works of his craft by the most approved authors, so that their contents and contrasts would be to him as the multiplication tables to a top form schoolboy or "Fowlers"[29] to a mechanic. As to working conditions, these could be in accordance with the most favourable interpretation of such by the International Labour Organization. Say 40 hours per week, with Christmas Day, Boxing Day, Good Friday, all public holidays and at least seven consecutive days' holiday in every year. Workshops clean and well ventilated, designed for comfort and so equipped as to eliminate waste of time, energy and fatigue. If in the course of his sorting the dirt and rubbish he comes across some discarded spiritual jewel or bric-a-brac, these he may be permitted to trade or keep for his own spiritual advantage or swap with his mates. No doubt his existing charter will cover any difficulty about the question of his clients being always right. If not, modern business efficiency would indicate the method of bringing it up-to-date. These conditions would secure his standard of life, give reasonable leisure for the cultivation of higher things, the practise of religion; soundly based on the accepted principle that the client, customer or public is the chief or only legislator in the work of the labourer. It is sometimes said, with what truth it is difficult to estimate, that the labourers in this sphere are very conservative in their outlook, yet the depersonalisation of labour in other spheres seems to have been accepted by many of them without protest. Be this as it may, should some public-spirited but prudent individual suggest to one or more of these spiritual dustmen that it would be to their and everyone else's advantage for them to adopt the methods of working and the conditions as outlined above, he would be met with a volley of words and missiles such as are seldom met with outside a dustman's collection.

Consider next in order, that noble profession the nursing of the sick. This by its very nature calls for a considerable amount of refuse collection and disposal. Patients, unable to perform this work for themselves, rely upon their nurses to do it for them. This calls for self-sacrifice in a high degree and the profession is one which still retains public estimation as a vocation, which means an all-round job. No one will dispute that much care and attention has been given to bringing the work of this profession up to the standards demanded by the necessities as well as the greater knowledge of the times. Yet although our hospitals and infirmaries tend to become a more and more congested world in themselves, where the isolation of the work of refuse collection and disposal would seem to offer all the supposed advantages claimed for it in other spheres, yet here again no one has suggested it desirable that it become a full-time occupation.

Coming down to earth, the farm provides another example of a life where refuse disposal is of everyday necessity. Of vital importance in its economy and essential to its very existence, where a tradition at least as old and a literature at least as extensive, as that of the spiritual dustman exists. Again the making of such disposal a full-time job is repugnant to its followers.

In contrast to the examples given above, urban civilisation provides a curious *volte-face*. Whereas the spiritual dustman integrates his work with a strong admonition to his clients to avoid in future further accumulation of rubbish and so eliminate his necessity as far as possible in this work, the urban dweller so lives as to make the dustman an ever-growing necessity. Whereas the nurse in the collection and disposal of refuse integrates this with the primary work of making the patients fit to do it for themselves, the urban dweller regards it as normal to be continually in the position of a patient in the matter. Whereas the farmer utilises his refuse in accordance with tradition and science, thereby enhancing the fertility and drainage of his land and the wear of his roads, the urban dweller pays heavily to have his refuse removed, and pays again to have it brought back to him in the shape of patent fertiliser, sewage farm cabbage, cosmetics, or the 101 things which extraction makes possible. What isn't possible poisons the fish. That which normally should be of value in the economy of the homestead is discarded and despised.

From what has been said it will be seen that refuse collection and disposal is a normal activity of man, tending to wholeness or holiness when integrated with the main activities of life, but repugnant to nature when not so integrated. Where, as in urban life, the work is a full-time occupation, it will nearly always be found that the labourers in this work are recruited from, not necessarily the less intelligent, but from those whom the denial of the right of private property has affected most harshly.

The man is not necessarily degrading himself by doing the work. Society does this for him socially. It uses him as the exemplar of the lowest in contrast with the highest. The Duke and the Dustman. The civilization is degraded and degrading which necessitates it. Those who defend it may think that oppression of the poor is eliminated by a 40 hour week and a living wage; but their casuistry is dictated by the shirking of a duty–the self-discipline which disposal of one's own refuse entails. Wages and conditions are secondary to the recognition of the person in the labourer.

IX
Distributism
by S. Sagar

The *Weekly Review*[30] has for its background a certain social philosophy, a philosophy which is implied in its every paragraph, but which in recent years has only rarely been brought into the foreground.

There are good reasons for this restraint. One is the nature of those years. They have not been years in which men of wisdom and self-control would urge their fellows to change the whole nature of their economy; unlike the socialists we have not seen the national emergency as the opportunity for us to get our own way. Another reason is that we have not wished to weary readers with "the same old and old o'er again." And a third reason is that there is a danger in indulging the delightful pastime of discussing detailed plans when you have no materials with which to build. The danger is that you may become involved in fruitless debates and even quarrels, debates and quarrels which would largely settle themselves if you could only get a start on the job. I submit that we have been right in largely employing our energies to explain the plan of another building that is being erected, right in trying to show our contemporaries that this building is not a home for the "common man," (building homes seems to be a knack men have lost) – not a home for the "common man" but a prison.

This attitude is often condemned as negative, mere fault-finding, and the rest. It is not so; it is not negative to persuade men that they are indulging illusion. Moreover, behind this critical attitude is the aforesaid positive philosophy of our

* *This chapter is taken from "Distributism," serialized in* The Weekly Review *in six parts, Oct. 17–Nov. 28, 1946.*

background which is a fresh wind of reality blowing across the fœtid intellectual atmosphere of our time. To dissipate that atmosphere is a difficult task and one which the impatient, practical man may disdain as not "showing results." Nevertheless, it is a first and foundational step to any results which will make for a return to saner and more human things.

So much in defence of our present attitude.

Now, however, there would appear to be a widespread feeling amongst readers that the time is ripe for something more definite, that there is a wide audience desiring to hear the things said which we are saying and that some attempt should be made to reach this audience. As a prelude one correspondent asks for a series of articles giving the simple outlines of Distributism. I do not think I have any particular qualifications for the job, but old Distributists, who will remember how well the job has been done before, will perhaps bear with me if I say that I am doing it by editorial request. I will endeavour to repress my personal whims and confine myself to the lines of orthodoxy.

Before coming to grips with my task I think it will help to prepare the ground if I comment on a remark which the correspondent made about the name Distributism. She does not like it. Neither do we; we have always recognized its clumsiness, but the difficulty is to find another and more attractive name which adequately expresses our objective, the objective of distributing economic power.

The root of the difficulty is that Distributism is not an "ism" in the sense that that term is understood today. That is, it is not something like a new opening in chess which a few clever men have perfected in the seclusion of a library or academy. It is not some new variation in sociology. It is an organic thing, a thing that was growing before men were under the unhappy necessity of discovering that there was a subject called sociology. It was the mark of European life for centuries; it was taken for granted by the men who founded the New World. Our tragedy today is due to the fact that it never fully matured;

but amidst all its imperfections, its tangle of feudal legality and the rest, the thing itself, the peasant and the guild, the reality of personal ownership of the means of production as the determining feature of economic life–that is clear to any man of insight.

The immediate point here, however, is that it seemed such a normal thing that men did not think of naming it until it had been destroyed. Even then only a few men saw it so clearly as to think it worthy of a particular name. The majority of its impoverished heirs did not see it. They were dimly conscious that they had lost something and sought to recover their loss by inventing a subject they called sociology. They studied this subject with such desperate zeal that they got into the state of mind which regards the normal as an anachronism, a state of mind in which they could not distinguish one way of going on from another unless the ways were described by words ending in "ism." So the clear-sighted few had to bow to the fashion; they had to find a name for the normal, human thing that they were supporting. The name they found was Distributism, and until someone can find a better name we shall have to be content not to change it–like the Conservative Party. At any rate, I do not propose to change it in these articles, but I want at the outset to distinguish Distributism from the modern "isms" whose advocates in one breath tell us will herald the coming of the Kingdom, and in the next tell us that we shall have to accept them because the alternative is universal death. It is not that sort of thing at all: it is a thing men once desired and failed to achieve through greed.

To complete this introductory matter I want to repeat that the principles of Distributism have been outlined before and to advise the newcomer to get hold of three short books. The first is Belloc's *Servile State*. This is one of those rare books which endure though they say things which men do not want to hear. They endure because they are carved out of hard material by a keen-edged tool of still harder material. *The Servile State* appeared at the moment when Socialism had triumphed amongst the intellectuals and it was, and is, the acid test for the Socialists. The fact that they have never answered it, but only ignored it, shows discerning men that what animates them is not a burning desire for a better way of life for the masses, but a burning desire for their own way. The other two books are Chesterton's *Outline of Sanity* and Belloc's *Essay on the Restoration of Property.*

The student will find these three much more instructive and much more entertaining than these articles. In fact, the best thing these articles can do for him is to send him to those books.

II

THE ROOT of the trouble is that man on the earth is in exile. Or, lest the materialist should suspect theology in this phrase, let us say that man on the earth cuts a funny figure. He cannot crop the grass as it grows, nor find an adequate shelter beneath the trees. In order to live he has to resort to the highly entertaining but highly dangerous adventure of meddling with nature. He must carry this meddling to such lengths that he and his fellows must come to some arrangement about it, otherwise they would be getting into each other's way even more than they do at present. Moreover, to make any marked success of the meddling man must also have access to the results of previous meddlings: to produce bread he must have a store of bread, and so on. Here again this calls for some arrangement with his fellows.

That is to say, man, in order to live, requires access to natural resources (Land), and to an existing store of the means of life (Capital).

Further, he must have some arrangement about the control of these two things: for I need not delay about the "free-for-all" dream which sustained some of the simpler of the early socialists, the dream that every man would always feel so good-natured, that every man could help himself to anything anywhere. Some arrangement there must obviously be, and to make such an arrangement is one of the reasons why man forms communities. On reflection it will also be obvious that the number of arrangements possible is strictly limited and that this number cannot be increased by any new discoveries in sociology, accountancy or currency manipulation. Every society must make laws to govern the control of Land and Capital, and, whatever variations and exceptions be allowed in practice, those laws must work from one of three principles.

The law might start by frankly recognizing two classes of subjects, vest the control of Land and Capital (by means of direct ownership) in the first class and compel the second (the dispossessed) to labour at the will of this first class. That arrangement was the mark of the pre-Christian world, where it was carried to its logical conclusion–the first class not only owning the means of life but also the bodies of the second class. It is known as Slavery and its sounds intolerable. But it might be salutary for us to remember that it was not found intolerable. I think it would be safe to say that men were as contented with it as men are with nineteenth century capitalism, or even as men are with twentieth century socialism. Be that as it may, two things about it are certain; the first is that it delivered the goods; it produced wealth, luxury and magnificence on a scale which now seems fabulous: and the second certain thing is that it endured. It endured because its practice was not a glaring contradiction of its theory: to persons dispossessed of economic power it did not offer the fiction of political power.

Another principle from which the law can start is to say that there shall be no individual ownership of Land and Capital, that these are to be controlled by the community and that the individual should work on them as directed by the community. If the thing were as simple as it sounds it would mean the de-personalization of man. He would become a creature of a group impelled merely by instinct, like the ant. Fortunately, it is not so simple as it sounds. In practice, as everyone knows, that abstraction called the community means the political officers of the community. A community cannot direct how every field is to be cultivated or where every house is to be built, any more than a community can drive a bus. The arrangement will leave a few men with the opportunity of decision and responsibility, that is, with the opportunity to develop personality. The danger is that they may develop unpleasant personalities. However, the germ of this arrangement was in Feudalism, as is evidenced by the legal theory that the king owned all the land and that the vassals held it only in trust. But feudalism didn't work out that way. The supreme manifestation of the theory is to be found in present-day communism under which a few party bosses control all Land and Capital and forcibly direct the labour of millions. How that will work out no man can yet tell.

The third principle from which the law can start is that all its subjects should exercise control of Land and Capital by means of direct family ownership of these things. This, of course, is the principle from which, until yesterday, our own law started. It was the theory of capitalism under which all were free to own, none compelled by law to labour. Unfortunately, in practice, capitalism largely diverged from this theory. In practice the many had no opportunity of obtaining Land and Capital in any useful amount and were compelled by physical necessity to labour for the fortunate few who possessed these things. But the theory was all right: Distributists want to save the theory by bringing the practice into conformity with it. Distributists want to distribute control as widely as possible by means of direct family ownership of Land and Capital. This, of course, means co-operation amongst these personal owners and involves modifications, complexities and compromises to which I will come in due course. But the aim is family ownership of land, workshops, stores, transport, trades, professions, and so on.

But to keep to the immediate point. I submit that the three arrangements – control by the few with legal compulsion to labour for the many; control by the State with legal compulsion to labour for all; and control by the many by means of ownership are the only determining, stable arrangements which a community can make about Land and Capital.

Moreover, Distributists regard it as very doubtful whether even the second arrangement is a stable one, whether Communism is not merely a transition to the old institution of Slavery. After the populace has become reconciled to the loss of freedom it is possible that State control may break down through inefficiency. Our bureaucracy is still largely engaged with words and figures, collecting and distributing paper tokens, but already there are signs that as it swells it becomes more muddled, signs which do not promise well for its tackling of real work; for real work cannot be done unless full responsibility can be exercised by men who are near to it. A possible development of State control is that the leading political officers might decide to convert their privilege into property; that the commissars for the counties might decide that they could manage the counties better if they had no interference from head office, that is, if they owned the counties. And by that time owning the counties would mean owning the men inside the counties.

I should like both our friends and opponents to note this fear of ours even if they do not share it. We fear that State ownership of "all the means of production, distribution and exchange" is a mere illusion, an illusion that will lead men back to the half-forgotten reality of ownership of man by man. But even if this fear proves groundless, even if State ownership proves to be a permanent way of going on, we still say it is a bad way, a way baser than belongs to man. We say that it will produce a society of individuals lacking initiative and responsibility, that is, lacking intelligence and personality. I should, I say, like friends and opponents to note all this; it explains things in us which they find inexplicable. It explains why we look sharply at machinery, why we are lukewarm about Social Credit[31] and its proposal to restore freedom by a new system of double entry. It explains, in short, an attitude in us which they consider obscurantist. The truth is we fully recognize the difficulty of restoring freedom by restoring property, we recognize it so fully that we fear it cannot be done without tears. But we are prevented from giving up the task as impossible because we see the alternative as so ghastly.

III

Family ownership in the means of production so widely distributed as to be the mark of the economic life of the community–that is the Distributist's desire. It is also the world's desire. There have indeed been a few men, generally men who have viewed their fellows from public platforms or through library windows, men divorced from realities, who have argued against the ideal of small property. There are also considerable numbers of men today who are uninterested in ownership (largely because they are hopeless about it), and assert that what they want is a secure income unharassed by the responsibilities of ownership. These latter have never thought things out, have never seen that a society cannot give security of income to its individual members without destroying freedom. With these men we can do nothing but continue to try and persuade them to think things out.

But the desire for ownership is still widespread. It is my experience that few men attack the ideal. The vast majority of men who argue against Distributism do so not on the grounds that it is undesirable, but on the grounds that it is impossible. We say it must be attempted, and with these men, too, we must continue to emphasise the results of not attempting it. We must do so because our primary task is to stimulate the will to attempt it.

But these men have a right to ask us for something more: they have a right to ask us to be candid about the difficulties of Distributism.

I must pause a moment here to have a clear understanding with the reader. My commission is to outline principles, and in coming to the difficulties that hinder those principles in practice, I shall continue to confine myself to outlines. I am not rewriting *The Restoration of Property*. That work goes into the mechanics of the job of attempting to restore property, into the details of the tactics to be followed. Here I propose to discuss the general aspects of the difficulties. *The Restoration of Property* starts from the assumption that the will to restore ownership is present. My object is to enliven that will by showing that a society whose mark is ownership is not impossible, nor even so difficult as many imagine.

For instance, I shall not concentrate on the machine, the mere mention of which is expected to reduce us to silence. For the machine is not a general difficulty: it is an incident, a particular example of the general difficulty. The general difficulty embraces the machine; it is an idea in the mind of man. And the difficulty is made more difficult by the fact that that idea is ninety per cent illusion: an illusion to which men have been prone in all times and are particularly prone in our own time; the illusion that the large unit of economic power is always and by the very nature of things more efficient than the small. Now if the difficulty were all illusion things would be simpler. But it has a root in reality, the reality that concentrated power can achieve things which the small unit cannot attempt; so that to limit the concentration of power looks like limiting the capacity of man—looks like what our opponents, in a phrase which sounds much less resonant than it used to do, called delaying the progress of civilization.

We have therefore to (1) endeavour to dispel the illusion, and (2) consider how far we need compromise with the reality.

As to (1) we must refuse to be mesmerized by the machine. As I have said, the machine is an example of concentrated power; indeed, it is now a weapon of the power but it did not create that power. That power was a threat to freedom before the machine existed and will continue to be a threat to freedom even if the machine prove to be merely an ephemeral phenomenon in the story of man. The steam engine did not, as I once heard a man say, "put an end to freedom." I do not know enough about steam engines to know whether a small steam engine would have been a practical proposition, but I know enough about the men of the eighteenth century to know that they did not want small steam engines. That was not the idea at all: the throb of the small steam engine would not have shaken the smallholder handloom off his holding. If the steam engine destroyed freedom, why didn't electrical power and the internal combustion engine restore it? Obviously these are suitable for small units, yet they have been used to concentrate the power of monopoly.

Again, we shall refuse to be satisfied with the mere assertion that the big unit is more efficient. We shall insist on examining results. In the primary matter of food, for instance, it has been repeatedly asserted that the big farm was more efficient than the small. But the results are not confirming that assertion. Indeed, results suggest that the "bonanza" farming which once captured the imagination of Bernard Shaw[32] which he hailed as the coming thing destined to exterminate the backward and degraded peasant, has now joined the host of nineteenth century lost causes and forsaken beliefs and impossible loyalties. The soil of the bonanza farms is now drifting down the drain, and, in spite of Mr. Strachey's[33] casuistry civilized men are poorly fed, and in spite of Mr. Dalton's[34] promises of jam tomorrow if we will only be patient whilst he follows the old Whig financial policy, all the prospects point to their continuing to be poorly fed.

It is the same with the assertion that the chain shops and the big stores are more efficient than the owner retailer. There has been no economic law-making for those concentrations of power. What has been at work has been human greed. The host of shop owners have not been turned into shop walkers, that is, into servants, by any "economic necessity"; they have been so turned by methods which are, to say the least, doubtful, methods which would not have been tolerated in a more civilized society. The fact is that over a very large field of human activity the big unit has no real advantage over the small. The illusion that it has is one that [it] itself fosters. Indeed, the fact is that the big unit, after a certain point, the point when it becomes too big to be grasped by one mind, becomes an inefficient instrument in the production or distribution of wealth. It is frustrated by complexity and by the incapacity to harness the wills of men.

So much for (1), for what I have called the illusion part of the difficulty. The conclusion is that there is nothing in the nature of things to hinder family ownership over a large area of wealth production and distribution. The obstacle is in the mind of man.

With the real difficulty I will deal in the next section.

IV

I SAID, in my last article, that the difficulty confronting us was the big unit of economic power, that much of this difficulty was imaginary but that it had a basis in reality.

Now our first business is to see the imaginary part for what it is. We must refuse to be bullied by the modern confusion of "economic law" with physical law. Economic law is a euphemism for the mood of men, and in our day that mood has been determined by greed. There was, for instance, no law making for that amalgamation of breweries which was a feature of the early years of the century. Beer can be brewed as cheaply and as well in small breweries as in large. And the same is true of most of the amalgamations which have been a mark of industry throughout the lives of most of us. They have been inspired either by greed or the equally doubtful motive of calling in the public to share the declining fortunes of industry. The same motive is at work behind the propaganda and pressure of the bankrupt industrial cities to rope in more and more of the surrounding urban and rural areas. In a word, very much of the boosting of the "efficiency" of concentrated economic power is defensive; it is a mask to hide the features of concentrated economic power; for those features now have about them that indefinable but unmistakable cast, the name of which is death.

Nor will this cast be changed by going in for bigger and bigger amalgamation, and calling it nationalization.

I submit, then, that much of our present centralization of power is not only unnecessary, it is also harmful, and if a start is not made soon to decentralize it we shall drag down the whole economy of our country.

But what of the real difficulty? There are cases where the large unit is more efficient; there are cases where it is necessary, in the commonsense meaning of that word.

In such cases we are prepared to compromise. Our scheme is not one of mechanical perfection; we are not hidebound doctrinaires. If our Minister of Health found (I don't think he would, but this is a supposition)–if he found that Distributism was standing between thousands of families and shelters, he would for the time being forego his heart's desire of helping men to build their own houses. It is true he has an advantage over our present Minister of Health in this matter. He would know that men would not lose the desire to own their own house because he had provided them with a temporary shelter to rent, whereas Mr. Bevan[35] fears that if men were encouraged to build their own houses–well, who knows where it would stop on the road to ownership.

However, we should, I say, compromise with reality. But before we did so we should want to be sure that it was reality and not mere semblance with which we were compromising. We should not be satisfied with the present fashion in "costings." If the large unit was proved more efficient, then our next step would be to weigh the material advantages against the spiritual disadvantages. If, for example, all the material costs of modern large-scale production, the capital outlay, the overheads, workers' play times and amenities could be properly figured and compared with older and more human methods of production, I suspect many moderns would have a shock. But even if it did prove more efficient, we should still ask whether the lower cost of the resulting product was worth condemning men to the deadening task of standing by a chain belt.

But there are cases where the large unit is clearly necessary. Mines and railways, for instance, cannot be started without large accumulations of capital. Here our first principle should be to prevent the unit being larger than sense and circumstance dictate. Physical fact necessitates a considerable concentration of economic power to work one coal mine; but physical fact does not necessitate the nationalization of mines. It is not beyond the wit of man to devise some scheme by which the several mines could be owned by chartered guilds of the miners who work them. In the case of the railways there is perhaps a stronger case for nationalization, though our experience does not suggest that amalgamation of the railways makes for greater efficiency. But here again the chartered guild is preferable to nationalization. In fact, nationalization should be regarded as the last resort. The State has sufficient indirect power over life without giving it direct power. Moreover, the State servant has practically no power of reaction against the State.

Here I can imagine a die-hard Distributist saying: "All this is futile: whatever expediency you adopt with the large unit, whether nationalization, the guilds or some revision of company law as sketched by Mr. Paul Derrick[36] in recent issues of the *New English Weekly*[37]–whatever expedient you adopt involves the representative system, and the representative system is moribund." That is true; but I would urge that the reason why the representative system is moribund is that it is today used by men divorced from property, that is from responsibility. But in a society marked by ownership, it would, I think, be a very different thing. In such a society the individual miner or railwayman could, I think, enjoy the illusion of ownership, and the small shareholder in a concern could have the same experience. In fact, in such a society even if a little nationalization here and there were found to be necessary or desirable, it would do no harm.

This is the feature I would emphasise. We wish to change the modern attitude towards production; but we are not perfectionists. We want the big unit to be regarded not as the desirable haven, but to be tolerated as an exception. We want to make family ownership in the means of production the characteristic note of our economy, but we do not visualize every man working his own land or his own business. It is the broad lines we are anxious about; provided we can get those clear we shall be very charitable towards the details. In our society we shall suffer poets and artists, players and playwrights and humbler types of vagabonds, men who do not feel the joys of ownership and find its responsibilities a handicap to their vision of less ephemeral things. We shall not only suffer them, we shall suffer them gladly, because when we meet them we shall know that we are still living in a free society. Neither do we visualize the abolition of every wage earner. But we do visualize the abolition of a class of wage earners, a mass of wage earners who have lost the hope of ever being anything else.

V

MEN TODAY seem to have lost the knack of confining a subject to a limited field. They listen not so much to what you say as to what they thought you should have said. For instance, at the beginning of these rough and hurried notes I made it clear what I was not doing. I made it clear that I was not doing the very thing that Mr. Henry Meulen[38] accuses me of not doing; I was not outlining "proposals for practical steps to implement the ideal of an industrial property-owning democracy." I repeat, (for in such circumstances one can only fall back on repetition), that task has already been done in *The Restoration of Property*. I repeat that that essay was written by Mr. Belloc in response to numerous accusations that Distributists had nothing practical to suggest. But the point that the author emphasized was that the preliminary to any of these steps was the creation of the will to take them. My chief object in these articles has been to stimulate the will; to give the newcomer to the subject a general idea of what Distributism means, especially to give him a sharp idea of what the absence of it means. In brief, I have been endeavouring to persuade men that Distributism is the only solution consonant with freedom to the strain which our economy suffers.

I do not think I was called upon to deal with other solutions which are in the field, even though many of these may be considered as allies of our solution. I have, for instance, not touched upon the great question of Social Credit with its numerous able, enthusiastic and in some cases almost fanatical supporters. This is not because I minimize its importance, but because I think that its effect would depend almost entirely on the mood of the society in which it was introduced. Social Credit is a proposal to distribute income, which is quite different to the distribution of property. It would not necessarily lead to the distribution of property. You could have a reasonable distribution of income in a society which had lost freedom. If Social Credit is regarded as a first step by men whose vision is to distribute property it would probably help. But too many Social Credit advocates of my acquaintance seem to regard it as the alpha and the omega: they give me the impression that after they have distributed income they will be able to go home to tea.

Again, I think Mr. Meulen has made out his case for abolishing the Bank Charter Act. But I am rather surprised to find him describing the abolition of that Act as "a practical step." It is a step which he has been trying to take all his life and has not succeeded. He has not succeeded because he is working against the mood of his time. A step may be easy to take if you can reach it, but if it is so far up the ladder that you cannot reach it then it is surely a misuse of language to call it "practical." Mr. Meulen's practical step is no more practical than are the numerous steps outlined in *The Restoration of Property*; the preliminary to both is to create in men a desire to take them. The same is true of Mr. Paul Derrick's proposals. He is impatient with the impracticability of Distributism, but his own scheme, however admirably he details it, turns on a revolutionary alteration of the company law. I think he will have a lot of propaganda spadework to do before he persuades men to agree to that. If you are sailing down the coast of South America in a doubtful barque in very dirty weather it is nice to draw detailed plans of the pleasant cruise that is awaiting you in the Pacific. But I have never understood why the men who indulge in these plans should be regarded as practical; especially have I never understood why they should regard as unpractical men who say: "Hadn't we better leave all that for the moment and concentrate on getting round Cape Horn?"

Our Cape Horn is the persuasion of men. I do not want to discourage men of affairs from formulating practical schemes, but I do want to impress on impatient men that we cannot suddenly change our society into a Distributist society by a cunning dodge. In the mood of our time any remedy that involves only "a stroke of the pen" will either be a fallacious remedy or we shall not be allowed to hold the pen. Before our proposals can be practised they must be discussed, and hitherto the Capitalists and the Socialists have combined to prevent them being discussed. That is, they have combined to prevent them being discussed on any national scale; they have combined to prevent them reaching the mass of men; they have combined to represent us a romantic medievalists, to dismiss us as one of those cranky family parties of which our jolly world is so full.

It may be argued that the inadequacy of Distributists is partly responsible for the success of this boycott, but, upon my word, I do not see what more we could have done. Death and old age and infirmity have taken toll of our champions but we have endeavoured to make our small voices carry as far as possible. We have also endeavoured to make them as sane and pleasant as possible. We have varied our approach; unlike the Hyde Park orator–Charlie I think his name was–we have not made the same speech every week. I think we are justified in claiming that we have combined two things which are not easy to combine: we have avoided boring intelligent men and we have kept the flame alight. Moreover, we have looked for no "careers." Our only hope has been that a day would come, a day when men would be compelled to return to the consideration of reality.

That day has come. It may be too much to say that Distributism is going to be practised, but one may say with some confidence that at long last Distributism is going to be discussed. And the question which naturally presents itself to us is how can we best make our contribution to the discussion. I assume that Lt. Col. Hope's Third Party would mean a wealthy backing from somewhere and that is precisely the thing which in all our chequered career we have never been able to come by. But it does seem possible that without aspiring to become a political party some organization in the nature of the old League might be revived; something that would enable Distributists to meet and know one another and enable them to make their presence felt in the Conservative Party, or at least open up a wider field for the spread of our ideas. I leave these matters to men more conversant with affairs, but I should like to conclude these articles by touching very briefly on one or two features of the prospect which were not present when, nearly forty years ago, Belloc and Chesterton sought to dissuade their friends of the Liberal Party from following the line of least resistance and embarking on the Fabian policy of "Social Reform."

VI

I SAID last week that I wished to conclude by outlining certain features of the prospect which were not present when the Distributist thesis was first propounded.

In our endeavours to persuade our contemporaries of the truth of our proposals we have followed two main lines of approach, a positive one and a negative one. We have argued that our economy was something that was consonant to the nature of man, something that made men, men of initiative and responsibility, and that made a society full of virility and variety, a society charged with that indefinable but unmistakable air of freedom. That was our positive approach; our negative one was to urge that if our proposals were not adopted there would be an end of freedom; in Belloc's words, "If we do not restore the institution of property, we cannot help re-establishing the institution of slavery."

Now hitherto we have not been able to persuade men of the truth of this negative line. By men I mean here the mass of men. There are a number of intelligent communists who clearly understand it. They say, in effect, "Yes, we know where we are going; we also know where you want to go. But we believe you are pursuing a mirage: you cannot have stability and freedom." There are also a number of intelligent men of no political colour who see it clearly, but who shrug their shoulders and say that nothing can be done about it; the forces making for slavery are too strong, and so on. But the mass of men simply have not seen that civic freedom depends on the distribution of economic power. They have gone on concentrating economic power light of heart and without knowing what they were doing. They have argued on the lines on which a man once argued with me about *The Servile State*. That thesis, he said, may be difficult to refute in theory, but these clean-cut theories never work out in practice. Devices to protect freedom would be discovered as the threats to it appeared, and in any case Britons would never consent to servile conditions. Meanwhile, Socialism offered him the opportunity of doing good to his fellow man.

Now in 1910 it was possible for a man to talk like that without being either a fool or a humbug. In 1946 it is not possible. In 1910 he could console himself with the reflection that the danger was imaginary, at least, a long way off, and anything could happen before he reached it. Today the danger is towering over him and even if he still keeps his eyes shut he can feel its presence. This is the first feature to which I would draw attention. The danger of servitude is so great and so near that it is obvious to the meanest intelligence. This is evidenced not merely by the recent declaration of the Conservative Party, but also by the attitude of the more sensible leaders of the Labour Party. Some of these high-reaching ones who have held out with Marx so long untried are pausing now for breath. They are seeing now what they should have seen when they embarked on their careers; they are seeing that their doctrine means compulsory labour with all the dubious and inhuman shifts that that entails. Their position is a difficult one and its difficulty will increase with the years. Already this spectre of compulsory labour, like the cheerfulness of Dr. Johnson's[39] acquaintance, "keeps breaking through." The leaders of the Labour Party, torn between manhood and false doctrine, are naturally seeking to evade the question. But it cannot be evaded, and the more the process of nationalization proceeds the more impossible will it be to evade it, or mask it, or compromise with it.

This feature of compulsory labour will bring into sharp relief another changed feature. The sham fight between those blood brothers, Capitalism and Socialism, is ending and the real issue, which has been submerged for a generation, is clearly emerging. The real issue is between freedom and slavery. This does not mean that freedom will necessarily triumph; our proletariat may still elect to vote itself into slavery. But it should mean that our proletariat will have a chance of knowing what it is doing, that it will not have the excuse that it voted itself into slavery in its sleep.

Again, one of the most persistent and powerful charges that has been brought against us is that our Distributist economy would result in a lowering of that famous standard of living which so occupies the minds of so many excellent men. Now in 1910 that charge was powerful. The first decade of the century may be said to have been the high summer of the Industrial Revolution. Already there were signs of a certain loss of freshness, even then there were discerning men who said the thing could not go on. But it was clearly going on. The average wage earner had not much chance of ever being anything but a wage earner, but his wage was not paid in paper and he could do something with it besides exchange it for other forms of papers. He could get food, good drink, reasonable shelter and fuel to warm that shelter. Even in the eating houses frequented by the poor men there was an air which now seems to have been an air of largesse.

All that has gone. The Industrial Revolution is now clearly in its autumnal withering. The machine may go on, but our method of using the machine will not go on. The machine, as we have used it in bigger and bigger concentrations, is giving less and less service at higher and higher costs. It is failing to deliver the goods, especially the primary goods. There is even the darker doubt whether it is not even failing to produce the primary goods. The conflicting reports make it difficult for the ordinary citizen to decide on this matter. All he knows with certainty is that the goods are not here. And, as Jorian Jenks shows in last week's number, it seems more and more doubtful whether our traditional financial policy (so sacred to the Socialists) will get them here. Even the men who are boosting that policy do not sound very confident about it. Their moaning sing-song of austerity today and jam tomorrow fills you in the end with a very dreary feeling.

In short, all the signs suggest that Industrial Capitalism will have to keep very quiet about the standard of living. All the signs suggest that we are but at the beginning of an era of scarcity, an era in which the rule will be "If a man does not plant neither shall he eat." And the scarcity will not be conjured away by changing the name of Industrial Capitalism to Industrial Socialism. It will only be conjured away by a complete change in our attitude to production. For its cause is not a material cause. Its cause is the next, and last, new feature to which I would draw attention.

When the more intelligent of the capitalists backed the Fabian scheme of Social Reform they did so because they saw in it something that might save them from a revolt of the proletariat. What neither the millionaires nor their Fabian friends saw was that the danger to the whole set-up would come not from a revolt of the proletariat but from the lethargy of the proletariat. And it is a danger for which neither Socialism nor Capitalism has a remedy, for both Socialism and Capitalism corrode the springs of the individual will. Neither is compulsory labour with its secret police and other parasites a remedy; that is, it is not a remedy which will increase production. The only permanent remedy is the one we advocate.

To conclude: If there is anything valid in my vision of these things we are at the end of an era of make-believe and are moving into an era in which words divorced from reality will have to be compressed more and more and words related to reality given a chance of a hearing; an era in which questions which men had hoped could be left till Domesday press for answers; an era in which our society, endangered from without and within, will need the goodwill of its members, and by goodwill I mean not mere dreary acquiescence but enthusiastic support. Our proposals, difficult as they may seem, are the only ones that will meet the situation. And it is surprising how quickly men discover reality under stress; it is also surprising how they overcome difficulties when the alternative is death.

X
Talking of Food: A Simple Restatement
by Jorian Jenks

MOST OF US USED, PERHAPS, TO TAKE OUR FOOD A little too much for granted. So long as we got our three or four meals a day, we did not enquire too closely whence the food came or whether there was enough to go round. It was rather a shock when Sir John Boyd-Orr[40] (now Secretary-Designate of the new international Food and Agriculture Organization) told us in 1937 that "the diet of nearly one half of the population, though sufficient to satisfy hunger, is deficient for health."

This deplorable state of affairs, however, was generally ascribed to poverty and unemployment, for had not economists been scratching their heads for years over "the problem of over-production"? Few people seem to realize that if everyone had an income sufficient even for basic needs there would be, not "over-production," but considerable under-production. It was not, in fact, until the United Nations Food Conference at Hot Springs in 1943 made the first serious attempt to survey the world food situation, that the truth became manifest. The Final Act of that Conference stated, without equivocation, that "there never has been enough food for the health of all people."

It is thus abundantly clear that the foundations of our civilization are not going to be restored simply by schemes for providing full employment and social insurance. However necessary it may be to distribute purchasing power fairly and effectively, money-incomes are going to be of very little use unless there is a sufficiency of real wealth available for purchase.

---

* *This chapter is taken from "Talking of Food: A Simple Restatement,"* The Weekly Review, *April 4, 1946, pp. 16–7.*

Food is not just fill-belly. It is the first essential of life, and one for which there can be no substitute. Unless our diet is adequate both in quantity and in quality, health is soon impaired and the way opened to a host of ailments and diseases. As that eminent nutritionist, Sir Robert McCarrison, has pointed out, "food . . . is the paramount influence in determining man's general physical endowment, powers of endurance and resistance to disease;" or, to quote an old proverb, "we are what we eat."

By all accounts we, as a nation, have always had a reputation for hearty appetites and good living. But until comparatively recent times this good living was literally home-grown in the sense that nearly everyone lived on the produce of the fields and commons surrounding their homes, as of course, is still the case in many parts of the world. This food was no doubt, by modern standards, coarse and monotonous; but it was wholesome, and also cheap in the sense that there was no heavy middleman's charges to pay.

This primitive type of economy was shattered, first by the Enclosures which uprooted the peasants and smaller yeomen to make room for commercial farming, and second by the Industrial Revolution which gradually drew these "displaced persons" into the towns to form a proletariat. Thus the great mass of our people became dependent on every mouthful they ate upon their ability to earn the money wages with which to buy food grown and handled by others. During this transition period, hunger and malnutrition became, not just a temporary hardship, consequent upon a bad harvest, but the regular lot of millions of working folk.

Then, from the middle of the nineteenth century onwards, a further change began to take shape. The lead which we had obtained in manufactures, added to our maritime and mercantile enterprise, gave us an increasing ability to buy our requirements abroad. At the same time the new railways and steamships were unlocking the greatest treasure house ever known–the accumulated virgin fertility of millions of square miles of new territory in the Americas, in Australasia and in Africa. This vast stock of soil capital was rapidly "liquidated" as foodstuffs and other primary products. So that at the very period when our national purchasing power was steadily expanding, so also was the supply of wealth available for purchase.

This combination of circumstances not only made food cheap and abundant (though never cheap or abundant enough for the poor), but created a firm conviction that this stock of soil capital was inexhaustible–that there would always be "plenty more where that came from." It is this conviction, quite unfounded as events have shown, that has made us so casual about food supplies.

Another consequence of this commercial prosperity was that food came to be treated simply as a commodity–something to be bought cheap and sold dear, to be manipulated in price and composition according to opportunities for profit. Many of the applications of scientific knowledge to foodstuffs have, in fact, been directed towards increasing its utility as an article of commerce.

White bread, frozen meat, tinned foods and pasteurised milk, for instance, are not *better* foods than the natural products. On the contrary, it is widely acknowledged that they are less able to sustain life and promote vigour. This is because the natural processes of decomposition to which all organic substances are subject must be frustrated if such foods are to be made suitable for handling and storing in bulk. To achieve this end, the vital properties of the foods themselves have to be immobilized, or even (in the case of wheat milled for white flour) removed altogether.

Thus the expansion of trade and industry, while it certainly increased the quantity of food consumed, substantially lowered its quality. As Sir John Orr and David Lubbock[41] say in their book, *Feeding the People in Wartime*, "with the rise of industrialism in the nineteenth century, the diet of the working classes deteriorated." The descendants of the commoners who had tilled their own plots of land and kept their own cows and geese became dependent for sustenance upon stale, denatured foods that were in addition often badly handled in transit and badly cooked. This latter observation is not, of course, a reflection upon the British housewife; women with grossly inadequate kitchen and larder facilities, and often with too much other work to do, can hardly be expected to give food the attention it needs, even when they can buy enough of it. It is no wonder that working class diets have come to consist so largely of ready-processed foods and bought meals.

It must not be thought, of course, that science has confined itself to commercial problems. A great deal of disinterested work has been done during the last 100 years. Unfortunately nutritional research, like agricultural research, has suffered from over-emphasis on analytical chemistry.

At one time it was believed that food could be regarded simply as fuel for the human engine, so that food values and body needs were calculated in terms of heat–calories. This method is still used to some extent, but it was soon extended by the separation of food constituents into groups (proteins, fats, carbohydrates and so on) which have different functions in the body. Much more recently it has been realized that nutrition is not just a matter of consuming quantities of these constituents. We need, in addition, minute amounts both of certain minerals (such as iron, boron and manganese) and various complex organic substances which are difficult to analyse and assess, like the vitamins and riboflavin. Indeed, the more that is learnt about nutrition, the more clear does it become that our knowledge is still far from complete.

Improvements in diet have therefore up to now been confined mainly to attempts to make good the grosser deficiencies by quantitative means, that is, by the use of orange juice and cod liver oil, and so-called protective foods like milk and fresh vegetables to supplement staple foods that are admittedly imperfect. This policy has certainly done a great deal of good; but it can clearly never be more than *remedial*. It is, in fact, designed primarily to offset some of the defects of another policy which is fundamentally unsound–that of allowing our diet to be dictated by the economic requirements of trade and industry. Would it not be much better to go direct to the root of the matter and aim to achieve a good diet in the first place?

Of recent years a very important discovery has been made. It is that the healthiest people in the world are not, as one might imagine, the richer inhabitants of highly civilized countries, with all the resources of medical science at their command, but certain small primitive communities such as the Hunza tribe of the North-West Indian frontier and the islanders of Tristan da Cunha.[42] The isolation of these people has compelled them to live entirely on the produce of their own soils, which they must perforce tend carefully, not only by thorough tillage, but by the return to them of all the organic wastes of the community. By comparison, we are not only living extravagantly, but living at infinitely lower standards of health than we need to.

This discovery confirms the ultimate conclusion to which all research seems to be leading, though it is not yet fully worked out, namely that food is not just an assemblage of constituents, but a vital link between life in the soil and life in men. It follows that the nutrition of human beings, and the cultivation of fertility in the soil, are simply different aspects of the one problem. Before we can enjoy good health, the soil from which our food comes must be healthy, and its products must reach us, not only in adequate quantities but with their vital properties unimpaired.

This new development comes at a time when the food situation has become extremely serious. Taking the world as a whole, soil fertility has been declining for many years past, and in a number of cases has reached the point at which large areas of the soil itself are being lost by erosion. This state of affairs is due very largely to exhaustive and improvident farming methods, and these in turn, as in the case of inadequate diets, to preoccupation with trade and industry. There are few virgin tracts of fertile land left, and while populations (especially in Asia) continue to increase, potential sources of food are unquestionably contracting. This is a situation which cannot be set right by the increased use of machinery or chemicals for the extraction of crops; for it is the soil itself that must be conserved and restored to health – an immense undertaking.

Thus the conditions of the late nineteenth century are completely reversed. At a time when our ability to buy has been drastically curtailed, the food surpluses on which we used to depend have shrunk greatly, and are likely to shrink still further. Disregarding those clever advisers who tell us that it is "uneconomic" to grow our own food, we must develop to the full our own resources.

We are, in fact, being forced to do the right things—to devote to the needs of our people the excellent land with which our little island has been endowed. But it is of the utmost importance that we should do it in the right way, by treating the soil, not as a mine from which the greatest output must be obtained with the least effort, but as the living source of our own health and happiness, which must itself be given every care and attention. Otherwise the fate of past civilizations that abused their soil will be ours too.

XI
Common Land
by H. D. C. Pepler

THE POPULAR IDEA OF COMMON LAND IS THAT OF an open space over which the public may range at will in the same way as it walks on the high road, swims in the sea or sunbathes on the beaches. Very few consider that land, even for such limited uses, requires to be looked after; the tins, bottles, papers and other items of a picnic residue are, it is assumed, automatically interred by earthworms or left to serve as an invitation for another holiday party to spread itself on the same site; if cattle appear they must be shooed away, especially from a pond big enough to bathe in; and what fun if a cigarette end sets fire to gorse–always good for a cheerful blaze!

Some reflective souls, mindful of past injustices, are convinced that to enclose any Common land is to deprive Englishmen of their rightful inheritance; they see the enclosures of the past as acts of violence against divine law organized by landlords who did not hesitate at murder, rape and robbery in order to extend their boundaries and enlarge their parks that they might gamble with forests and stuff themselves with pheasants from their own man-trapped preserves.

In these views there is the sufficiency of truth both to account for exaggeration and give continuity to error. The public's rights are of but recent recognition and would not have been considered but for the congestion of the towns which puts a premium on the open space. A hundred years ago if one talked of a Common he would have been understood to

* *This chapter is taken from "Common Land,"* The Register, *June 1948, pp. 184–87.*

refer to land owned or cultivated in common, to which the public might or might not have access. The enclosures too often infringed personal rights, they almost destroyed peasant proprietorship in many parts of England, but no one objected that they prevented factory workers from basking in the sun.

The underlying pressure which led and leads to enclosure is the growth of the population and the necessity to feed it. I do not forget or exclude the motive of a landlord's greed; the evidence of avarice indicates a prior necessity. The demand for more land for sheep grazing in the sixteenth and corn growing in the eighteenth centuries was caused by the greater consumption of wool and corn–there were more backs to be clothed and more stomachs to be filled. Landlords took advantage of an existing necessity exactly as do lorry drivers of a petrol shortage; a black market is a more certain proof of necessity than it is of greed!

From Saxon times there have existed two kinds of land used in common, that which was ploughed and cultivated by farmers of a village on the strip system (of which an example remains at Laxton) and that which was called "waste"–valuable for hunting, fishing, firing, grazing and litter cutting. It is with the latter I am now chiefly concerned. Many such wastes became known as Commons and their proprietors as Commoners because the rights to hunt, shoot, graze, etc, thereon were enjoyed in common by a limited number of individuals. As an owner of such rights on one Common of which I have been Reeve[43] since 1918, I may be allowed to illustrate the matter of personal experience.

Our rights are appendant, that is attached to a house or a piece of land from time immemorial, and were, until recently when he sold his land to pay Death Duties, shared with the Lord of the Manor (his right like our own being attached to named and specified fields in the Parish). We have the right to graze cattle, to shoot, to fish, to firing, litter, etc., over some 600 acres marked off by the furrow of a plough, contours of the land, tracks, way leaves and existing farm boundaries. The rights may not be alienated from the land to which they are attached except, by custom, to other land in the same Parish.

This was the kind of common which has suffered under the acts of enclosure since Plantagenet times when the Lord of the Manor was allowed to enclose as much of the waste as he pleased for tillage etc., provided he left sufficient of the Common for such as were entitled thereto. Francis Bacon[44] later on is to write of the "due care taken that the poor Commoners have no injury by such improvement," and "improvement" is an operative word because land held in common does not receive the same care and cultivation as that given to the meadows and arable under the eye of a farmer in his own homestead. This common land served an economic purpose nevertheless, for though it produced less than it would were it divided up for individual cultivation, it had the nature of a capital reserve to be drawn upon in emergencies. Such land may be common, but, agriculturally speaking, if it is unclean it may be required to be made clean – in order to be more productive of food; and necessity tends to taken precedence over rights established in more ample times.

Land is a live thing which will deteriorate in value unless it is kept in being. There are in fact a number of Commons which have reverted to waste simply because they have not been productively used. That is the danger with which ours is faced. Up to the beginning of this century the land was more or less kept in good heart by the demands made upon it, sheep grazed in the Downland, cows and bullocks the lowland, gorse (at one time encouraged for the fire of an adjacent brick kiln) and bracken were cleared in the winter for litter. The wool merchant, the dairyman and the butcher translated our produce into food and clothing. But this happy balance of power had already been threatened by the economic trends of the Victorian era; with the arrival of New Zealand mutton and Australian wool, sheep-rearing had begun to be uneconomical and, with the war (1914–1918), sheep and their shepherds disappeared from the hills, the grass grew coarse and tangled by neglect until it was burnt. At the same time farmers found themselves under-manned; for other reasons also they were obliged to reduce their herds, the demand for grazing on the lowland fell off, the gorse and bracken extended their area of growth, bushes grew (useful only to gypsies for hanging out their washing), the Commons showed signs of return to its primitive waste–and what could be done about it?

One element in the deterioration was the motor car, for not only is the main road through the Common a bye-pass to Brighton but it was widened and cemented by the County authority into the appearance of a race track. From less than sixty vehicles a day passing through there are as many in half an hour, mostly driven by motorists with inhibitions about gate closing; fatal accidents to man and beast, once unknown, have now to be counted among our risks.

The pressure upon agriculture to produce more food is bound to increase and the obvious first duty of the farmer is to make the best use of his land. The best use to which our Common land can be put is to make fuller use of the rights we and our predecessors have exercised since time immemorial, by cultivating the land so that it may grow more grass and carry more cattle.

Our main difficulty is financial. We hold lands not money in common; possibly only once in our long history have we ever been capitalists and that was when we were graciously pleased to allow the London Brighton and South Coast Railway to stretch its rails across us in 1846 and a sum of £200 was accepted in compensation–a sum invested in Consols and not exhausted upon improvements (pond dredging, ditch cleaning, tree planting and fencing) until a few years ago. The hire of the "Looker" (so called because he looked after the cattle) and other out of pocket expenses were met by charging for the use of extra grazing rights and, recently, by a levy on the Proprietors of 10 shillings on leases used by themselves. The only way in which the Proprietors can acquire any surplus income is by letting more cattle onto the Common which they cannot do until the Common is cleared bit by bit and reseeded–an expensive business.

We are embarked in an essay in joint ownership in which the profit, to the members individually, has never been measured in terms of cash, any that has accrued collectively has been absorbed in the care of the land. The Proprietors will continue that policy; the more we put in, however, the more we shall be able to draw out–ultimately there should be a surplus in excess of what the land will take back, and that surplus could be declared in terms of money. Does that mean a share-out among the Proprietors?

My view is that a new order of knighthood should be created and Knights of the Land be appointed to preserve all Commons, including road wastes and other neglected corners of the countryside against all comers . . . . I see a great gathering of Stewards, Bailiffs, Reeves and Rangers from the Forests, Fens, moors and mountains of England assembled to receive a great charter, but that is a story for a later issue.

Notes

1. A kind of manual first assembled by George Bradshaw (1801–1853), who grew up in the Railway Age in England, when new railway companies and lines were proliferating. He saw the need for a book that would inform travelers of the times of the trains. Thus in 1838 he issued the world's first railway timetable in book form, published monthly and costing 6 pence. It was an immediate success; its final number was published in June 1961. For the men of Victorian and Edwardian England, a "Bradshaw" was part of everyday living.

2. Alfred Harmsworth (1865–1922). Better known as Lord Northcliffe, he purchased his first newspaper, *The Evening News*, in 1894 and turned in sufficient profit that he went on to found the *Daily Mail* in 1896–and which is still one of the major British tabloids. He was, and is, widely regarded as the man who began the dumbing-down of newspaper readerships, by including in his paper innovations such as sports pages, "human interest stories," a women's section, and the large banner headlines. He once said, "when I want a peerage I will buy one"–reinforcing the belief of many like Chesterton and Belloc that peers were largely created *by* and *for* money. Even a man of limited intellect, David Lloyd-George, described Northcliffe as "one of the biggest intriguers and most unscrupulous people in the country."

3. Pietism. A movement that arose within the ranks of Protestantism during the seventeenth century. Although many names are associated with its rise, it was largely the zeal of Philippe Spener, a pastor in the German Lutheran Church, that gave it substance. He organized private assemblies in people's houses for the purpose of pious reading and mutual edification. He styled these meetings "Collegia Pietatis"–hence the name Pietists. Over time the movement went off on many theological, mystical, and devotional tangents so that the doctrine became ever more heterodox, but many within Protestant ranks saw the Pietists as nothing more than "sanctimonious hypocrites."

4. The Canterbury Festival. Takes place annually in the county of Kent in England. It was inaugurated just after the close of World War I by the Anglican Archbishop of Canterbury. It was, and still largely is, dedicated to promoting the cultural arts in their many forms, with emphasis upon classical concerts, choral singing, drama, and various forms of popular entertainment. It still draws large crowds.

5. *From a Cornish Window.* A novel by Sir Arthur Thomas Quiller-Couch (1863–1944) published in 1906 in London by J. W. Arrowsmith and in New York by E. P. Dutton.

6. Sir Robert McCarrison (1878–1960). Studied Medicine at Queen's University, Belfast, and upon graduation was posted to the Northern Frontier by the Indian Medical Society. His research there on goitre earned him widespread recognition, and led to his 1928 appointment as Director of Nutritional Research in India. Studying vitamin structures and disease patterns on the sub-continent, he demonstrated that many of the common diseases found in modern Western

society were due to defective diets occasioned by food processing. His work on the deleterious effects of chemical additives, white flour, and canned foods–well ahead of its time–was widely published by the medical press, but he was ignored by both his profession and the government. His main work, *Nutrition and Health*, is still in print, and his pioneering work is carried on by the McCarrison Society for Nutrition and Health in England.

7. *Quem deus perdere vult, prius dementat.* "Whom the gods wish to destroy, first they drive mad."

8. Felidi. Alternatively rendered as Felidæ. The biological classification for the cat family.

9. Genevas. This is Lymington's scathing reference to the League of Nations, founded in 1920, and based in Geneva. Designed to be an organization that promoted world peace and conflict resolution in the wake of WWI, it became a toothless talking shop. It was eventually disbanded in 1946, and the United Nations came into being.

10. Charles Bathurst (1867–1958). He entered the British Parliament as Conservative MP for South Wiltshire in 1910. During WWI he served as Parliamentary Secretary to the Ministry of Food and was raised to the peerage (as Baron Bledisloe) in 1917. He later served as the Parliamentary Secretary to the Ministry of Agriculture and Fisheries (1924–28). He became Viscount Bledisloe in 1935 upon his return from New Zealand where he was (from 1930) governor-general.

11. Edmund Blunden (1896–1974). Described by American author, Paul Fussell, as a "poet, scholar, editor and man of letters." Having fought at Passchendale in WWI, and obtained the Military Cross for bravery, he was a passionate War Poet who sought to convey *all* of the different aspects and emotions of war. He was a close friend of poet, Siegfried Sassoon. His *The Shepherd* earned him the Hawthorne Prize in 1922. He was Professor of English Literature at Tokyo University (1924–27) and a Fellow of Merton College, Oxford (1931–43). He was awarded the Queen's Medal for Poetry in 1956. Although he is best remembered for his work *Undertones of War* (1928), it is generally agreed that his many works on the English countryside were his finest.

12. William Cobbett (1766–1835). Born to poor parents in Hampshire in England, he rose to be one of the most famous polemical journalists of his day, his reputation being based on his fearlessness and his profound integrity. At a time when Catholics were still being persecuted in England, he found the courage to write that "the Protestant religion had been established by gibbets, racks and ripping knives," though Cobbett himself was *not* Catholic. His weekly journal, *The Political Register*, was a "hit" with the English downtrodden of the time, and gave birth in 1830 to a compilation work called *The Rural Rides*, to which Massingham refers frequently. *Cottage Economy* appeared in 1821–22 and was aimed at showing country labourers how they could improve their situation through practical self-help: bee-keeping, bread-making, keeping cattle, pigs, and poultry, and so on. It is still immensely popular.

13. Dr. W. G. Hoskins (1908–1992). An English local historian who founded a Department of Local History at Leicester University–the first of its kind. His particular contribution to this study was his demonstration that human activity

had a deep impact on the English landscape, a thesis that he outlined in his pioneering work *The Making of the English Landscape* (1955). Leicester University still honors his contribution with an annual Memorial Lecture.

14. Laxton. A town in Northamptonshire, England, that to this day preserves its "open field system." It was also, perhaps not coincidentally, the site of an intentional Distributist community of at least five families living on 77 acres, and seeking together to restore Christian rural life by rejecting industrialism and pursuing self-sufficiency. It was begun some time after 1935 under the leadership of John Hawkswell, who some years before was instrumental in attempting to establish a similar community at Langenhoe in Essex on a 1500-acre estate.

15. Joseph Arch (1826–1922). Son of a Warwickshire farm laborer who co-founded the National Agricultural Labourers' Union in May 1872; it grew within two years to some 86,000 members. As its first President, Arch was invited by the Canadian government to visit the country to see if he thought it suitable for large-scale British emigration. Over the next few years, as a result, the Union assisted some 40,000 laborers and their families to move there. He was elected Liberal Party MP for North-West Norfolk in 1885, and remained in Parliament until 1900.

16. Sir Daniel Hall (1864–1942). An eminent agricultural reformer. He was, at one time, President Secretary of the Board of Agriculture and Fisheries, but his main fame came from his Directorship of Rothamsted Agricultural Research Station, which was founded in 1843 by John Lawes. He was also Director at the John Innes Institute, and on the Trades Union Congress Scientific Advisory Committee. An expert on Tulips, he wrote *The Tulip* (1929), *The Cultivator* (1934), *There is no Over-Production* (1934) and *Reconstruction of the Land.*

17. Long Ashton Research Station. Established in 1903 as the National Fruit and Cider Institute by farmers and growers who sought solutions to their problems, it became in 1912 a Department of Bristol University, and its scope was extended to horticulture, food science, crop nutrition and physiology, and crop protection. In 1987 it was merged with Rothamsted Experimental Station and Broom's Barn Experimental Station to form the Institute of Arable Crops Research, and is now known simply as Rothamsted Research.

18. Cockney. Strictly speaking this is a person born within the sound of Bow Bells in East London, England, but with time it has generally come to refer mainly to people in East London *as a whole.* Cockneys evolved a peculiar English dialect of their own known as "rhyming slang"–such as "apples and pears" meaning "stairs."

19. Peter Drucker (1909–2005). An Austrian educated in England who obtained his doctorate in Public and International Law in Frankfurt in the 1930s and became an economist with an international bank in London. In 1937 he moved to America where he taught Philosophy and Politics. For the next 20 years he was the Professor of Management at the Graduate Business School of New York University. A writer of over 30 books–dedicated evenly to management on the one hand and to politics, economics, and society on the other–he was described by *Business Week* as "the most enduring management thinker of our time."

20. Elstree Film Studios. Set up in 1914 by early film-makers Percy Nash and

John East, at Borehamwood, Hertfordshire, England. It was a convenient location: close enough to London to enjoy the necessary facilities of the city, but far enough away to avoid the downside effects. It was for many years the center of the British film industry, though of late years it has been experiencing a certain renaissance.

21. John Cadbury (1802–1889). A Quaker who sought to bring his religious beliefs into the running of his business as an attempt to bring harmony to worker and employer relations. He began selling tea and coffee in 1824, but by 1831 he had moved into selling cocoa and chocolate. It is still an enormously successful company with its main factory still located at Bourneville near Birmingham, England. A "Bourneville" was also one of the company's most popular chocolate bars.

22. Walter E. Elliot (1888–1958). A Scottish Conservative MP who entered Parliament in 1918. His war-time experiences led him to adopt a Tory paternalist view of the world. As a result he inaugurated the National Housing Company to build prefabricated "Weir houses" in the slums of Clydeside. He was also the first to introduce free milk for school children. Between 1932–when he became a Cabinet Member–and 1940, he was variously Minister of Agriculture, Scotland Secretary, and Minister of Health. A voracious reader of anything from histories to horticultural manuals, he was blessed with a powerfully retentive memory, and as a man of ideas was thought to be of Prime Ministerial calibre. Today, however, his name is barely remembered.

23. A reference to William Ralph Inge (1860–1954), English Anglican religious leader, Platonist, and author. He was Lady Mary College Professor of Divinity from 1907 to 1911, and became Dean of St. Paul's Cathedral, London, in 1911, remaining there until 1934. Known for his pessimism, he was referred to as the "Gloomy Dean." His works include *Christian Mysticism* (1897), *Personal Idealism and Mysticism* (1907), *Mysticism in Religion* (1948), and *Diary of a Dean* (1949). He was frequently the butt of G. K. Chesterton's attacks.

24. Arthur David Ritchie (1891–1967). Prof. Ritchie was educated at St. Andrews and Cambridge, and held the Chair of Logic & Metaphysics at Edinburgh University from 1945 to 1960. He was a frequent contributor to *Mind*, *Philosophy*, *Analysis*, and *The Philosophical Quarterly*. His works include *Scientific Method: An Inquiry Into the Character and Validity of Natural Laws* (1923), *The Natural History of Mind* (based upon the 1935 Tarner Lecture on the Philosophy of the Sciences that he delivered at Trinity College, Cambridge), *British Philosophers* (1950), and *Studies in the History and Methods of the Sciences* (1958).

25. Bertrand Russell (1872–1970). Celebrated Welsh philosopher who wrote prolifically on logic, the theory of knowledge, and the foundations of mathematics. A grandson of the infamous Lord John Russell, he studied at Cambridge and then entered the Royal Society in 1908. He won the Nobel Prize for Literature in 1950 and was the founding President of the Campaign for Nuclear Disarmament in 1958. His works include *Principles of Mathematics* (1903) and *An Introduction to Mathematical Philosophy* (1919).

26. *Respice finem*. Latin for, literally, "look to the end." The full proverb is *quidquid agas, prudenter agas et respice finem*; i.e., "whatever you do, do prudently, and look to the end." In the context, the phrase constitutes advice to look ahead

and consider the ultimate results or outcome.

27. Sophocles (495–405BC). An Athenian playwright who, thanks to the wealthy background of his family, was enabled to study all of the arts. His first entry in the annual "Theatre of Dionysus" competition brought him First Prize, beating the renowned Aeschylus. There followed 120 more plays, of which 18 won first prize. From this large output only seven have survived, of which it is generally agreed that *Oedipus the King* is the best. His play *Antigone* tells the story of a passionate young woman who refuses to submit to earthly authority when it forbids her the decent burial of her brother, Polyneices. It is a play which highlights the drama of the conflict between the claims of the State and those of the individual conscience.

28. Pimlico. In Hagreen's day this was a residentially very select area of central London, and it is still characterized by many streets composed of imposing Victorian and Edwardian houses. In the context Hagreen is playing upon the New Testament text, "A man went down from Jerusalem to Jericho." Jerusalem is regarded as the temporal City representing Heaven, and Jericho represents Hell. Pimlico, therefore, in spite of–or *because* of!–its bourgeois spirit was "hell" for Hagreen.

29. Fowlers. A manual similar in a way to a Bradshaw (see note 1, *supra*). Aimed at mechanics–professional and amateur–it was a book of maintenance and repair, available for most every model of car, and which combined description with diagram so as to facilitate a mechanic's work.

30. *The Weekly Review*. The successor journal to *G.K.'s Weekly*. When G.K. Chesterton died, in 1936, Hilaire Belloc was engaged to fulfill the editorial duties on the paper. Belloc's natural distaste for such work led his son-in-law, Reginald Jebb (1884–1977), and Hilary D.C. Pepler (1878–1951) to take on the editorship; in 1938 it was decided that a name change was in order, and *The Weekly Review* was born. It ceased publication, as such, in June 1947. Notwithstanding Harold Robbins's great contribution to the Distributist cause, it might reasonably be said that he was somewhat unfair to *The Weekly Review* in saying in *The Last of the Realists*, his biography of G.K. Chesterton, that it had ceased to be a Distributist publication. Even in its last year of publication–an heroic effort in itself given the economic, political, and legal pressures of WW II–the contributions of Hilary Pepler, S. Sagar, Jorian Jenks, L.J. Filewood, Rex Tremlett, E.H. Haywood, and other veteran Distributists are still to be found, defending with gusto Distributism and related points of view.

31. Social Credit. The theory devised by Major Clifford Hugh Douglas (1879–1952), who, as a trained engineer, believed that prices had to be liberated from the cost of production by subsidies. Advocating a National Dividend within a Leisure State, his main work of exposition is *Economic Democracy* (1920). Most Distributists, like Penty, Stirling Taylor, Titterton, and Chesterton, never believed in the Douglas Scheme, though a minority of Distributists, like Maurice Reckitt, believed that it was compatible with and complementary to Distributism. For his part, Fr. Denis Fahey wrote: "Though many, including the present writer, do not agree with Major Douglas's Social Credit scheme of reform of the monetary system, nobody questions his knowledge of the financial world."

32. George Bernard Shaw (1856–1950). Irish playwright, author, and 1925 Nobel Prize winner who became a Socialist on hearing Henry George speaking about Land Nationalization. Joined the Fabian Society, writing the Fabian pamphlets *Socialism for Millionaires* (1901) and *Fabianism and the Empire* (1900). Other works include *John Bull's Other Island* (1904), *Man and Superman* (1902), *St. Joan* (1923), and *Too Good to be True* (1932). He once declared: "The middle and upper classes are the revolutionary element in society; the proletariat is the conservative element."

33. John Strachey (1901–1963). Became a Labour MP in 1929, but resigned in 1931 to join the New Party founded by Oswald Mosley. When Mosley founded the British Union of Fascists in 1932, Strachey did not follow him, probably because he was part Jewish. Indeed, Strachey became a dedicated anti-fascist. In 1936, along with Harold Laski and Victor Gollancz, he formed the Left Book Club to promote socialist ideas and anti-fascism. By 1939 the Club had over 50,000 members. The Club's most important published work was George Orwell's *The Road to Wigan Pier* (1937). Strachey was Minister of Food in the Atlee government from 1946 to 1950.

34. Hugh Dalton (1887–1962). Son of the chaplain to Queen Victoria, he studied at Cambridge University before becoming a Labour MP in 1924. Between 1931 and 1935, he taught at the London School of Economics, following the loss of his parliamentary seat. In 1940 he was appointed the Minister for Economic Welfare by Winston Churchill, and in 1942 President of the Board of Trade. In 1945 he became Chancellor of the Exchequer, and in 1946 he nationalized the Bank of England. He wrote *Practical Socialism* (1935) and *Call Back Yesterday* (1953).

35. Aneurin Bevan (1897–1960). Welsh Far Left Labour MP who became one of the most important Ministers in the 1945–51 Labour government. He was appointed Minster of Health in 1945 by Clement Atlee, and was responsible for setting up in July 1948 the National Health Service (based on *free* access for all), as well as the system of General Practitioners around the country. He resigned in 1951 when the Labour government introduced dental charges. He became Deputy Leader of the Labour Party in 1959.

36. Paul Derrick (1916–1996). An advocate of economic co-operatives, he was called a "Christian Socialist" by many people after WWII. A correspondent of Maurice Reckitt's and a contributor to Jebb and Pepler's *Weekly Review*, he wrote (among other works) the *Co-operative Approach to Socialism* (1956) for the Socialist Christian League and edited, with John Francis Phipps, *Co-ownership, Co-operation and Control: An Industrial Objective* (1969).

37. *The New English Weekly*. Founded in April 1932 by Alfred Richard Orage (1873–1934), with a masthead reading "a review of public affairs, literature and the arts." It sought both to explore politics and to espouse the Social Credit theories of Major C. H. Douglas. Orage's fame is still associated, however, with his long editorship of *The New Age* whose "Golden Age" was 1910 to 1914 when it was an influential magazine drawing contributions from many of the best upcoming minds of the day. Editorship of the *Weekly* passed into the hands of Orage's disciple, Philip Mairet (1886–1975); it lasted until ca. 1949, although Mairet was an Anglican Christian and not a "spiritualist" like Orage.

38. Henry Meulen (1882–1978). Monetary reformer who advocated what he called "Free Banking" in his 1934 book of the same name. The editor of *The Individualist*, he also wrote *Banking and the Social Problem* (1909), *Industrial Justice Through Banking Reform: An Outline of a Policy of Individualism* (1917), and *Individualist Anarchism* (1949). He was also a writer for the *Weekly Review*, and he contributed a chapter, along with Joseph Labadie, to the French-language book, *Diverse Aspects of Anarchism.*

39. Dr. Samuel Johnson (1709–1784). English author, poet, essayist, critic, and journalist. An eminent literary figure, he is best remembered for the fact that he was the first (in 1755) to compile a comprehensive dictionary of the English language. A friend of Edmund Burke and Oliver Goldsmith, he co-founded with them the Literary Club. His other major contribution to the arts was the *Lives of the English Poets* which was published in ten volumes between 1779 and 1781.

40. Sir John Boyd Orr (1880–1971). A Scottish graduate in Medicine and the Biological Sciences, he became the head of the Nutrition Institute in Aberdeen in 1914 and transformed it completely in the ensuing 25 years. In 1929 he wrote *Minerals in Pastures and their Relation to Animals*, and he founded and edited the *Nutrition Abstracts and Reviews* in 1931. In the 1930s, his interests turned to humans, and he wrote the 1936 report "Food, Health, and Income." Through his Directorships he became an immensely wealthy man, giving his money for the 1949 Nobel Peace Prize to the "World Movement for World Federal Government." He wrote *Food and the People* (1943), *Food: The Foundation of World Unity* (1948), and *The White Man's Dilemma: Food and the Future* (1953).

41 . David Miles Lubbock (1911–1992). Graduate of Cambridge University and son-in-law of John Boyd Orr (1880–1971), appointed by the Carnegie Institute (U.K.) in 1937 to gather material together in a dietary and clinical survey which sought to correlate the relationship between health and diet. The survey came to an abrupt end in 1939 when war broke out. As a result, much of the material collated for the Institute was used in the book that he later co-authored with his father-in-law, *Feeding the People in War-Time* (1940). Lubbock also worked with the Food and Agricultural Organization (1946–51) where he was for a time Orr's personal assistant.

42. Tristan da Cunha. A small island of roughly 50 sq. miles located in the South Atlantic ocean. It is some 1,300 miles from St. Helena and 2,000 miles from the Cape of Good Hope in South Africa. Named after its Portuguese discoverer, Tristão da Cunha, in 1506 it was known as "remotest island in the world," yet it is almost wholly self-sufficient in spite of its many material disadvantages.

43. Reeve. The chief official in a manorial, local, or village council.

44. Sir Francis Bacon (1561–1626). A Renaissance courtier who at the age of 12 had gone to Cambridge University. It was there that he turned against Aristotelianism and Scholasticism in favour of Renaissance Humanism. He entered Parliament in 1584 and advanced under King James I, becoming Viscount St. Albans and Lord Chancellor of England in 1618. He liked to see himself as an apostle of a new methodological interpretation of the universe, and outlined his views in *The Advancement of Learning* (1605) and *Novum Organum* (1620). Other authors have seen the influence of Kabbalism in his work. He is regarded by many as having laid the foundations of the modern world.

About the Authors

The following brief sketches are provided for interested readers who wish to acquaint themselves with the lives and characters of those among the loosely connected group of men making up the Distributist Movement of the 1920s, '30s, and '40s who are featured in this Volume of Distributist Perspectives. *Their widely varied careers, backgrounds, talents, and achievements are an eloquent testimony to the depth and seriousness of the Movement.*

DOROTHY SAYERS (1893–1957)

DOROTHY SAYERS was the daughter of an Anglican cleric and was one of the first women to receive a degree from Oxford University, whence she graduated in 1915. She then joined Blackwells, the publishers, as a copywriter. Her first novel, *Whose Body?*, published in 1923, created the now celebrated figure of Lord Peter Wimsey, who was to appear in another 14 volumes of short and full-length stories. In her day she became the doyen of crime writers, though she had an unfailing admiration for the work of E. C. Bentley and G. K. Chesterton.

In 1936, however, she changed direction and moved into playwriting, producing *The Busman's Holiday*. A complete success, it led to her being inundated with offers of work. This included *The Zeal of Thy House*, produced for the 1937 Canterbury Festival, and *The Emperor Constantine* for the Colchester Festival in 1951. She penned the now famous *The Man Born to be King* in 1942, and it was broadcast on the BBC's Children's Hour to great effect.

She also produced a popular translation of Dante's *Divine Comedy* in English, and was an accomplished poet, theologian, and apologist. Her numerous works also include *Creed or Chaos?: Why Christians Must Choose Either Dogma or Disaster* and *The Lost Tools of Learning*. She enjoyed the friendship of T. S. Eliot, Charles Williams, and C. S. Lewis. She was also a popular circuit lecturer, whose motto was: "The only Christian work is good work—well done."

ERIC GILL (1882–1940)

ARTHUR ERIC ROWTON GILL was an engraver, sculptor, typographer, and writer. He was trained as an architect in London and also took classes in writing and illumination at the Central School of Arts and Crafts. Inspired by well-known calligrapher Edward Johnston, who was himself an admirer of William Morris and later a member of the Ditchling community, Gill acquired a passion for lettering that remained with him for life.

His professional career thus began with carving letterforms in stone for numerous tombstones and memorials in and around London. This work further led to a series of stone sculptures exhibited in galleries, as well as others executed for the BBC Headquarters (such as *Prospero and Ariel*), the London Underground, numerous churches, and various war memorials, among which is the WWI memorial at the University of Leeds which depicts a powerful Christ driving modern-day money lenders from the Temple. He also produced the magnificent Stations of the Cross that are still to be seen in Westminster Cathedral in London, and designed St. Peter the Apostle (Catholic) Church, located in Gorleston-on-Sea, Great Yarmouth.

As a type designer Gill produced *Perpetua* and the companion italic *Felicity*, *Gill Sans*, and *Joanna*, the latter named after his daughter. The majority of his type designs were done for Monotype Typography, a company still in existence. In 1931 Gill produced his influential *Essay on Typography*. As an engraver and illustrator, much of Gill's notable work was produced for the Golden Cockerel Press, established in 1920 and owned and directed from 1924 to 1933 by engraver Robert Gibbings. The Press was one of the most renowned English private presses of the early 20th century, and its books served as outlets for the wood engravings of numerous well-known engravers, including Gill, Gibbings, David Jones, and John Buckland Wright. The most famous work to result from the Gibbings-Gill collaboration is the 1931 book, *The Four Gospels*. Along with Gibbings, Gill was a founding member of the Society of Wood Engravers, which was formed in 1920. Among the many engravings and illustrations that he produced are *The Song of Songs*, *The Passion of the Lord Jesus Christ*, and *Troilus and Criseyde*. He also produced numerous wood engravings for bookplates and posters.

Gill was also the founder (with Hilary Pepler) in 1921 of the Guild of Saint Joseph and Saint Dominic at Ditchling, a village in Sussex, England, where Gill lived from 1907 to 1924. His apprentice Joseph Cribb went with him to Ditchling; fellow craftsmen and their families followed later on, including Edward Johnston (1912) and Hilary Pepler (1915), and their families. Another early member of the Guild was the painter and poet David Jones. Some consider Pepler's Saint Dominic's Press to have been in some respects the heart of the Guild. Even after Gill left Ditchling for Pigott's farm, he continued to train pupils and assistants, and his legacy inspired a generation of stone carvers and letter cutters. His apprentice remained at Ditchling, taking over the stone carver's workshop, and the Guild numbered among its members in the 1920s craftsmen such as carpenter George Maxwell, weavers Valentine Kilbride and Bernard Brocklehurst, and wood-engraver Philip Hagreen. In 1932 the silversmith Dunstan Pruden (who taught Capt. Herbert

Shove the trade) joined, followed by artist and engraver Edgar Holloway. The affairs of the Guild were not wound up until 1989.

As a thinker, social critic, and art philosopher, Gill expressed the life that he had attempted to lead at Ditchling and thereafter. His ideas on art and philosophy were influenced by the work of French Thomist Jacques Maritain, whose work *Art and Scholasticism* was published by Gill in 1923 as the first-ever translation of Maritain in England. Gill's works of philosophy and social criticism include *Art and Love*, *Art and Prudence*, *Art and Manufacture*, *Clothes*, *Money and Morals*, *Beauty Looks After Itself*, *Work and Leisure*, *Work and Property*, *Christianity and the Machine Age*, and *It All Goes Together*.

His faithfulness to the Catholic social vision is best illustrated by noting a remark that Pope Pius XII made when he happened upon one of Gill's books: "This man has understood our encyclicals." Gill was a remarkable man, himself a convert to the Catholic Faith in 1913, who combined theoretical erudition with manual dexterity to a high degree, thereby influencing an enormous range of people that included Catholics and non-Catholics alike. Not a few of his contemporaries considered him to be remarkable for his holiness; Fr. Brocard Sewell, the English Carmelite, in fact remarked of him that "he represents my ideal of the holy man. . . . [For] the saint. . . is the man who loves God and his neighbor with all his heart, and Eric did that to a degree I have seldom encountered."

Some commentators have suggested, based on the material presented in Fiona MacCarthy's biography of Gill, that because of his personal failings his ideas and work are today unworthy of appreciation. Fr. Sewell was not of this mind. Indeed his earlier judgment was not significantly altered (see Brocard Sewell, "Foreword," *Servile Labour and Contemplation* [Aylesford: The Aylesford Press, 1989], p. 13; those looking for a more in-depth assessment of the MacCarthy work, along with a consideration of Gill specifically in its light, would do well to consult the review by Fred Black, C.S.B., of St. Michael's College, Toronto, in the *Chesterton Review* [Vol. XVI, No. 1, February 1990, pp. 607–25]). "Times have changed," Sewell wrote, "and one may think him wrong on some points. Notwithstanding, he seems to me to be a great teacher, in the line of Ruskin and Morris, from whom we may learn much."

GEORGE MAXWELL (1890–1957)

George Maxwell was a Catholic layman, Third Order Dominican, Distributist, peasant proprietor, and carpenter who embodied in his lifestyle the ideals and attitudes that the Distributist League and the Catholic land movement were attempting to propagate. Originally a coach-builder from Birmingham, England, he was induced by Fr. Vincent

McNabb to join the community of craftsmen and Distributists in Ditchling, a village in Sussex, England, in 1922. Ditchling was "founded" by Eric Gill, Hilary Pepler, and Edward Johnston, originally from Hammersmith, who moved to the village from 1913 to 1916 for various reasons, but soon found themselves united in an effort of rural craftsmanship and communal life. Maxwell was a handy man, skilled as a carpenter, wheelwright, and loom-builder. When he came to Ditchling, he became a member of the Guild of St. Joseph and St. Dominic, established by Eric Gill and Hilary Pepler to foster Catholic craftsmanship in theory and especially in practice; for the Guild, "the principle of individual human responsibility being a fundamental of Catholic doctrine, and this principle involving the principles of ownership, workmen should own their tools, their workshops, and the product of their work." As one of the village's most skilled carpenters, Maxwell built his own carpenter's shop, in order to provide furniture and other objects for the community, as well as his own furniture for his home, the Ferrers.

During the 1930s he built his first loom, and in the aftermath of WWII he expanded this craft immensely, supplying art schools and workshops throughout England with looms. As an accomplished amateur builder, Maxwell built his own home at Ditchling and, along with the workshop for St. Dominic's Press, several houses that belonged either to the Guild–incorporated for business purposes as the Spoil Bank Association, Ltd.–or members or supporters living at Ditchling. A good friend of Harold Robbins, whom he had known since 1919, he lived the Distributist ideal, working in his company while managing the land and livestock on his smallholding.

Guildsmen such as Maxwell were required to be Third Order Dominicans; guild members met twice a day to recite the psalms and hymns of the Little Office of the Blessed Virgin Mary according to the Dominican rite, in the small chapel built near the workshops on the commons.

Maxwell was an extremely knowledgeable Thomist, and he knew many other major philosophers well, both ancient and modern. He was therefore considered to be Ditchling's "resident philosopher" and one of the deepest thinkers among the Distributists. His house was in fact the "principal port of call" for the men of the Guild to argue and talk over their ideas. He held rigidly to what Michael Sewell (later Fr. Brocard Sewell) calls the "stricter" school of Distributism, thinking even Belloc and Chesterton heterodox on certain points. As an illustration of his intransigence it may be pointed out that later in his life he began to disapprove of some of Maritain's philosophies, though the bulk of Distributist League members saw Maritain in the light in which St. Thomas saw Aristotle: as *the* philosopher.

Fr. Sewell relates in his memoirs that many of the younger Distributists who were faced with conscription for World War II consulted Maxwell for his assessment on a book on just war doctrine—which effectively implied the injustice of England's participation in the war—by the well-known German Thomist, Fr. Francis Stratmann. Maxwell's verdict was that he found Stratmann's position unimpeachable; as an illustration of Maxwell's sound grasp of the philosophy, others who shared his assessment of Stratmann's work were the English Dominican Fr. Gerald Vann, O.P., Fr. Francis Drinkwater, and the well-known English Catholic writers Donald Attwater, E. I. Watkin, and Eric Gill.

Maxwell contributed frequently to *G. K.'s Weekly* and *Cross and Plough*, the English Catholic Land Association journal. As a supporter of the land movement he contributed an essay on craftsmanship to the important anthology *Flee to the Fields*. He died in 1957, leaving his son, John, to continue the work at his shop.

H. J. MASSINGHAM (1888–1952)

SON OF THE WELL-KNOWN newspaper editor, H. W. Massingham (1860–1924), H. J. was a journalist, author, and one of England's leading natural historians and ruralists. During a rich life of activity, he contributed to papers such as *The Field, The Spectator, Country Life, The New Age, The Adelphi, The New English Review,* and *The Weekly Review.* In addition, he wrote some 40 books which covered the cultural, agricultural, and religious patrimony of England and made him the "Englishman's Englishman."

Beginning his career as an agnostic, working for his father on *The Nation* and for the guild-socialist *New Age*, he eventually came to affiliate with the Anglo-Catholic wing of the Church of England, probably under the influence of Philip Mairet and Maurice Reckitt. This move towards a specifically Christian view of life and society became evermore accentuated in his later writings, and eventually led to his conversion to Catholicism ca. 1940. For a time he was on the staff of the anthropology department at the University of London, working with its professor, Grafton Elliot Smith. In his later work on the craftsmanship of the English countryside, he accumulated an impressive collection of rural tools, now held by the Rural History Centre at the University of Reading.

A declared Distributist, he was involved in a number of bodies which propounded his view of the world: the Right Book Club, founded by Captain Jock Ramsey, MP; the Council for Church and Countryside; and the Soil Association, of which he was a Founding Member. He was also heavily involved in the Kinship in Husbandry group, which was active from 1941 to 1950, and was composed of agriculturalists and writers who together attempted to both formulate and propagate a vision of organic farming and a philosophy of husbandry. Its first clerk was Lord Northbourne, the author of *Look to the Land;* other members included the poet Edmund Blunden, the journalist Philip Mairet, the soil expert Sir Alfred Howard, the nutritionist Sir Robert McCarrison, and the historian Arthur Bryant.

Apart from his autobiography, *Remembrance*, written in 1941, Massingham's important works include *A Treasury of Seventeenth Century English Verse*, *Cotswold Country*, *Rural England*, *The Tree of Life*, *Wisdom of the Fields*, *Where Man Belongs*, and *Faith of a Fieldsman*. In writing the *Tree of Life*, he enjoyed the assistance of M. B. Reckitt, whom Massingham met through their mutual association with the Council for Church and Countryside. His leadership of the field in which he labored is illustrated by his having edited several volumes of essays, such as *England and the Farmer* and *The Natural Order*, which included contributions from important figures such as Viscount Lymington and Sir Albert Howard.

The significance of Massingham's love for English agriculture and its fine traditions of husbandry and craftsmanship are happily becoming more and more appreciated. Dr. Hilda Kean of Ruskin College at the University of Oxford has referred to Massingham as "the forerunner of the modern ecological movement, who looked to organic farming and the benign treatment of animals to create a new way of life." And Richard Moore-Colyer, a leading researcher of English Ruralism and Professor at the Rural Studies Institute of the University of Wales, wrote recently that "taken overall, the Massingham *œuvre* is characterised by a profound sincerity, a deep love of England and Englishness, and an omnipresent fear that the traditions which lay at the root of all he believed to be good about the English were under threat from a mechanistic economo-centric world in which the individual played but a minor role. Lyrical in description and pungent in criticism, Massingham's writing is refreshingly free of pedantry; the considerable learning is worn lightly and he manages to enthuse profusely without resorting to over-indulgence. At his best he bears comparison with the very finest ruralist writers, and in the literary celebration of the English countryside and its culture he probably has no twentieth-century rival. As a polemicist, meanwhile, he stands shoulder-to-shoulder with Cobbett (many of whose ideals he shared) although as a mild-tempered and gentle man he was entirely without the former's trenchancy and bombast."

HAROLD ROBBINS (1888–1954)

A Distributist, Catholic land movement activist, journalist, and editor, Harold Thomas Robbins was born in Birmingham to a Protestant family, and converted to Catholicism in the early 1900s, after briefly declaring himself a socialist, as many non-Catholic social thinkers did who were attempting to find a way to distance themselves from the prevailing Manchester liberalism. His conversion is most likely due to, among other things, his having discovered the two most prominent English Catholic writers of his time–Belloc and Chesterton–and their appealing critique of both socialism, about which he was having doubts, and capitalism.

Robbins jumped into the Distributist movement early, attempting unsuccessfully to write for the two weeklies then espousing it, the *Eye Witness* and its successor the *New Witness*. After military service in the First World War he became involved in the "New Witness League," founded in 1918 around the weekly for opposing corruption in politics. Robbins was made Chairman of the Birmingham branch, the most active branch of the league. The group's work focused ideologically on Distributism and the opposition to the eugenicist policies then being pursued by the British Ministry of Health. Some of Robbins's thinking on this topic is found in his *An Examination of Eugenics* (London: Burns, Oates and Washbourne, Ltd., 1930). In the spring of 1921 the league wound up its activities, and two years later the paper of the same name ceased publication.

In 1925 those collaborating on the *New Witness* gathered around a new paper, *G. K.'s Weekly* (to which Robbins contributed), begun in order to "promote and ensure the discussion of the real economic forces of the age under their real names," as Chesterton put it. Partly as a natural outgrowth and partly due to its financial straits (which it was in until the demise of its founder in 1936), and the need for subscribers, a league was also formed around this weekly, "for the restoration of liberty by the distribution of property"; or, the Distributist League. Robbins led, as Chairman, the Birmingham Branch of the league from 1926 to 1933, the most active and aggressive branch among some two dozen extant around 1927. He was chiefly instrumental in founding, with Msgr. James Dey, Rector of Oscott College and later Ordinary to the British Armed Forces, the Midlands Catholic Land Association; Robbins was its Honorary Secretary during the years that it was active, 1931 to 1936. This effort translated into practice what Robbins felt was somewhat of an overemphasis on mere talk: it was, he said, a "working model of practical distributism." He also edited the journal of the Catholic Land Associations of England and Wales, *The Cross and the Plough*, from 1934 to 1946, published by the Catholic Land Federation of England and Wales.

He co-authored with K. L. Kenrick in 1928 what came to be known as "the Birmingham Scheme," a pamphlet entitled *Unemployment: A Distributist Solution*; his friendship with Kenrick, who was the other chief mover of the Birmingham branch of the league, spanned many years. Kenrick called Robbins the "real power house" of the movement in their area. In 1946 he wrote a short biography of GKC–and also a history of Distributist activism from 1920 to 1940–dedicated to Kenrick and entitled *The Last of the Realists*, though it was not published until 1948, and then only serialized in *The Cross and the Plough* because of wartime restrictions on paper.

Robbins's short but powerful *magnum opus* was published in 1938 as *The Sun of Justice: An Essay on the Social Teaching of the Catholic Church*; he expressed its thesis thus: "Social Justice is crucial to the future of the Faith. There are many ways to the Faith, but it is certain that the concept of Our Lord as the Sun of Justice is not only valid, but is the only way by which our disillusioned and despairing world will return to Him" (pp. 10–11). Dorothy Day (1897–1980) noted in a 1954 issue of her paper, *The Catholic Worker*, that Robbins's *Sun of Justice* "contains the best thinking ever done on Distributism."

HILARY PEPLER (1878–1951)

A PRINTER, PUPPETEER, journalist, and Distributist, Hilary Douglas Clarke Pepler was born of a Quaker farming family in Eastbourne, Sussex; in 1905 he settled in Hammersmith, beside the Thames, with his wife Clare, where he was surrounded with arts and crafts history, such as William Morris's Kelmscott House. (May, his daughter, lived nearby.) The calligrapher Edward Johnston was a close friend and neighbor; Eric and Mary Gill were also in town until 1907, when they left for Ditchling village, in Sussex. Pepler was employed by the London County Council from about 1907 to 1915, working in child care; during this time he wrote *The Care Committee: the Child and the Parent* and *Justice and the Child.* Through the Fabian Society in London he saw much of G.K. and Cecil Chesterton and Hilaire Belloc. In pursuit of interests in hand-crafts and publishing, he co-founded the Hampshire House Workshops with the others of like mind in Hammersmith, providing Belgian refugee craftsmen with an opportunity to work at carpentry, embroidery, and shoemaking. The endeavor sprang from the Hampshire House Club for working men which he founded in 1907; the house was bought with help from Chesterton, Belloc, and others. Pepler's first publication was the 1915 *The Devil's Devices* (on machinery, and subtitled "Control versus Service") over the Hampshire House imprint, illustrated with woodcuts by Gill and calligraphically dedicated to G.K. Chesterton by Johnston. This collaboration with Gill resulted in Pepler's 1915 move to Ditchling village with his wife and three sons who were born in Hammersmith (Pepler's three daughters were born later in Ditchling): David, who would look after the family farm at Ditchling and marry Elizabeth Gill; Stephen, later Dominican priest (as Fr. Conrad) and author of *Riches Despised*, on the tension between industrialized man and the peasant faith of Christianity; and Mark, who was to take over Pepler's later publishing imprint in 1936.

The family moved into Gill's original house in Ditchling–Sopers–the Gills having by then moved into Hopkin's Crank on Ditchling Common. Pepler was baptized a Catholic by Fr. Vincent McNabb in 1916, after meeting the Dominican while visiting Hawkesyard Priory with Gill. Pepler then set up St. Dominic's Press, which, as a hand-press operation, incarnated for him the Distributist ideal which saw, with a primary attachment to the land, the art, economics, and philosophy united in primary hand-crafts. The Press produced some of the "liveliest and least pretentious pieces of hand-printing produced since the end of the fifteenth century" (Walters); his type was "worthy of ranking with William Morris' Kelmscott Gothic" (Hoehn). St. Dominic's produced over 200 books or pamphlets, including works by Fr. McNabb, Jacques Maritain, Raïssa Maritain, many illustrated by Gill and the other wood engravers and calligraphers at Ditchling such as David Jones, Desmond Chute, and Philip Hagreen.

In 1918 Pepler moved from Ditchling village into Hallets on the common, where carpenters, weavers, and sculptors soon joined the original contingent–Gill, Pepler, and Johnston–to pursue the life of rural craftsmanship that the "founders" considered to be the Catholic temporal and social ideal; officially the group incorporated as the Guild of Ss. Joseph and Dominic in 1921. Most were Dominican tertiaries who recited the office together at fixed times daily; Fr. McNabb acted as spiritual director. During these years Gill and Pepler collaborated in editing an occasional journal called *The Game: A Magazine*, which appeared from 1916 to 1923. It carried many illustrations from then or future members of the Ditchling community, including Philip Hagreen and Desmond Chute.

Later the Pepler's moved into Fragbarrow farm, still on the common, and Pepler's son David managed the small family farming operation there until he suffered an untimely death from tuberculosis in 1934. In 1924 Eric Gill left the guild and Ditchling due to a rupture with Pepler over various issues. The break grieved Pepler for a lifetime, but it was healed eventually through the efforts of Clare Pepler and Mary Gill who kept up correspondence and mutual understanding between the families; the marriage of Betty Gill to David before his death also helped resolve the breach. After the Gill's departure from Ditchling, Pepler and his family moved into their home on the commons.

Until 1936 Pepler continued his work with St. Dominic's Press; later he devoted himself to drama, as an author of mimes and an accomplished puppeteer. His mimed stations of the cross were performed in St. Paul, Minn., Santa Fe, N.M., and Pittsburgh, Penn.; his *The Field Is Won*, a mime of the life of St. Thomas More, was produced at a London theatre for celebrations of the canonizations of St. Thomas and St. John Fisher; he produced mimed versions of well-known plays for the *BBC*; and he took puppets from his own theater to the international marionette show in Liége in 1930.

His other works include *Plays for Puppets* (1928), *Pilate: A Passion Play* (1928), *In Petra* (1923), *Concerning Dragons* (1921), *Bethlehem: A Tableau of the Nativity for Presentation to Children* (1927) and *The Three Wise Men: A Nativity Play* (1927).

Upon Chesterton's 1936 death, he secured directorship and co-editorship, with Reginald Jebb (Belloc's son-in-law), of the *Weekly Review* (published thenceforth by the Ditchling Press, successor to St. Dominic's and managed by Pepler's son Mark and Michael Sewell), in all but name the successor to *G. K.'s Weekly*, organ of the Distributist League, which Pepler supported in the '30s as its honorary secretary. When the *Weekly Review* came to an end in 1949, Pepler established a small journal, *The Register*, which he published until his death.

Others of his works of commentary and social and art criticism are *The Hand Press* and *Pertinent and Impertinent*. Towards the end of his life, he wrote the invaluable *A Letter from Sussex: About My Friend Eric Gill* (1950), giving an insider's view of what it was like to work with the talented, if difficult, artist. Pepler's last public activity was his production of his mime, *The Passion of Our Lord*, performed in London, at Albert Hall. Following Pepler's death, his requiem was offered in the guild chapel at Ditchling, and he was buried there in the ancient parish churchyard, near his son, David.

Stanley B. James wrote of Pepler's writing that its "austere beauty" cannot be denied. "It is entirely free," he continued, "from superfluous ornament and sentimentalism. The intellectual quality is high; the lines are packed almost too closely with thought."

JORIAN JENKS (1899–1963)

JORIAN EDWARD FORWOOD JENKS was born in Oxford in 1899. He was the son of a solicitor and prominent academic and constitutional-history writer. Jenks was educated at Haileybury and Harper Adams Agricultural College in Shropshire, where he graduated with a National Diploma in Agriculture in 1920. Prior to further education at Oxford's Institute of Agricultural Economics, which granted him a B.Litt., he had experience as a farm manager in Berkshire and traveled to New Zealand, Canada, and Australia working, studying and lecturing. Following his time at Oxford, he spent a year as an agricultural lecturer in Devon, during which he married and took over the tenancy of Ecclesden Farm in Angmering, West Sussex, England.

Politically, Jenks was attracted to the only party at the time that supported his vision of home agriculture and national self-sufficiency in food, and joined the British Union of Fascists. (As John Phillips points out, writing for the Angmering villiage website [*angmeringvillage.co.uk*], "West Sussex was seemingly a hotbed of BUF activity and it probably drew the greatest support and sources of finance from the county.... These people were not the skin-head followers that today we rightly or wrongly associate with the BUF's successor, but respectable men, women and knights of the realm, many having become disaffected with the Conservative Party. They were not necessarily disloyal people–many had fought during WWI and others were to fight for their country against Hitler and his policies during WW2.") Jenks's knowledge and aptitude led to him being appointed the Union's agricultural advisor, in which capacity he developed its agricultural policy, articulated in his 1938 *The Land and the People*. He was also the driving force behind the BUF's Land Tithes war in East Anglia in the mid-1930s–a campaign that brought the Union considerable success amongst small farmers and agricultural laborers.

He was also a prolific writer on agricultural subjects in its publications; he had a weekly column in *Action*, for instance, until 1940. He advocated farming by organic methods and was convinced that many of the modern diseases, including the rise of cancer, were the result of the use of chemical fertilizers.

He was put forward by his party as the prospective MP for Worthing and Horsham, but no election took place due to the outbreak of war. Again according to Phillips, Jenks "was essentially a studious man and occasionally wrote to the local press answering criticisms of the BUF and insisting that they were a party advocating freedom and peace. [He] seems to have been a low-key candidate and appeared happy farming at Ecclesden and continuing his writing."

In May 1940 he was arrested and detained along with some 800 members of the Union under Defence Regulation 18b (1A), following the suspension of the Habeas Corpus Act in England. No records are available that indicate the reason for his detention. During his detention, Prof. Moore-Colyer believes, Jenks was subjected to uncompromising methods of interrogation at the hands of Britain's MI5 at its "notorious" Latchmere House. Later he was interned at Walton Gaol near Liverpool; as the subject of a 23-hour lock-in regime he became deeply depressed by the conditions at Walton, "where sanitation was primitive..., medical facilities vestigial, and food largely inedible." After his release in July 1941, Jenks moved back to his mother's house near Banstable, Devon, for the rest of the war. He became deeply involved with the Kinship in Husbandry, and in 1943 accepted editorship of the *Agricultural Bulletin*, produced by the Agricultural Section of the Economic Reform Club and Institute, founded seven years earlier and led initially by Kinship in Husbandry member Lord Northbourne. By 1946, when the *Bulletin* was renamed *Rural Economy* (its masthead read: "A non-party Commentary devoted to the development of a Sound National Economy rooted in the Soil") and circulated to members of Fordham's Rural Reconstruction Association (RRA), Jenks had also accepted appointments with the RRA, the Council for Church and Countryside (he served as secretary from 1945 to 1948), and the Soil Association. Jenks wrote the 1955 report of the RRA, *Feeding the Fifty Million*; the document carried an introduction by Laurence Easterbrook, agricultural correspondent on the *Daily Telegraph* and then the *News Chronicle*. He later became editorial secretary for the Soil Association, editing its serious journal, *Mother Earth*, from 1946 until his death. He wrote prolifically, contributing frequently to journals such as Reckitt's *Christendom* and Mairet's *New English Weekly*, and actively promoting his beliefs in organic farming and his view that Britain should be self-supporting in the production of basic foods.

When former BUF leader Sir Oswald Mosley formed his new Party, the "Union Movement" in 1948, it advocated European union and development of Africa by the principal European countries. Jenks did not favor this policy and did not join the new party. He wrote numerous books and pamphlets between 1950 and 1959, most of them advocating organic husbandry and better land use and decrying the exhaustion of non-renewable natural resources. He also returned to his earlier theme of health and nutrition and the dangers of chemical fertilizers and insecticides. His works include *Farming and Money* (with J. Taylor Peddie), *The Country Year*, *The Stuff Man's Made Of*, and *From the Ground Up*. Prof. Moore-Colyer notes illustratively that Jenks's books "Seem to cross the corporatist/organic divide" (*Agricultural History Review*, 49 (II), p. 196).

He died of a heart attack on August 20, 1963. According to Phillips, he has been described as a latter-day William Cobbett, while Prof. Richard Moore-Colyer noted that he, "together with others of the interwar Right, demand[s] our attention as [guardian] of the *flamma sacra* against what seemed at the time to be insurmountable odds."

K. L. KENRICK (1882–1975?)

DISTRIBUTIST, JOURNALIST, and Catholic Land Association collaborator, Kenrick was born in Denbighshire, Wales, in the early 1880s and became a schoolmaster, teaching in Birmingham. He was active in the circle around the *New Witness* and its corresponding league, and was one of the earliest thinkers and writers who worked out the doctrine of Distributism in the early 1920s, along with Fr. Vincent McNabb, Eric Gill, and Fr. John McQuillan. He succeeded Brian Harley as Honorary

Secretary of the Birmingham branch of the New Witness League–which had Harold Robbins, his chief collaborator, as its secretary–and served in the same post for the local branch of the Distributist League as well, which also numbered within its ranks others such as Father Austen Barker, O.P., along with Harley and Robbins.

With Robbins, Kenrick drafted in 1928 the pamphlet, *Unemployment: A Distributist Solution*, which ultimately became known as the "Birmingham Scheme." It was a visionary and practical document, explaining how the massive unemployment of the late 1920s could be resolved by the training and settlement of unemployed folk on the land as smallholders. This proposal became a milestone for the Distributist movement insofar as it represented a coherent and clearly articulated proposal, bringing Distributist ideas into practical realization. Altogether some 20,000 copies of the pamphlet were distributed. Its cost figures were updated in 1932, and a copy was distributed to every Member of Parliament and selected members of the House of Lords, though it had no influence on government policies. It continued to be updated through at least 1935.

Kenrick was a regular contributor to *G. K.'s Weekly*, as he was to the *New Witness* earlier on; he was, according to Fr. Brocard Sewell, held in "very high regard" by G. K. Chesterton. The works he produced for the Distributist League include *What is Distributism?* which was published in 1926 by the Distributist League in London in a pamphlet which included Chesterton's *The Purpose of the League*; and *The War on the Weak*, published in 1930. The latter was central to the League's anti-eugenics campaign. Kenrick also contributed a chapter–"The Case for the Peasant"–to the important anthology *Flee to the Fields*, which served as a manifesto for the Catholic Land Associations in England and Wales, which Kenrick supported with fellow Distributists Herbert Shove, Fr. McNabb, and Robbins. The book's importance can best be illustrated by comparing it to *I'll Take My Stand*, the manifesto of the American Southern Agrarians, and *Rural Roads to Security* and the *Manifesto on Rural Life*, the equivalent works for the Catholic "land movement"–i.e., the National Catholic Rural Life Conference–in the United States.

In 1958 the Birmingham Natural History and Philosophical Society published a short work Kenrick wrote for the centenary of the Society, subtitled "The records of the society and the story they tell." Robbins records Chesterton summarizing Kenrick's character and action thus in 1928: "Ah, Mr. Robbins, you have a great man at Birmingham."

PHILIP HAGREEN (1890–1988)

NOTED CATHOLIC WOOD ENGRAVER, illustrator, artist, and social critic. Hagreen studied as a painter in Cornwall and London. After trying a number of trades after World War I, he discovered wood engraving, and became, in 1920, a founding member of the Society of Wood Engravers. By 1922 he had moved to Ditchling and was learning letter cutting. He followed Eric Gill and his family to Capel-y-ffin, but stayed only for 18 months. He returned to Ditchling by 1932 and became a member of the Guild of St. Joseph and St. Dominic there, which was founded by Eric Gill and H. D. C. Pepler.

He focused thereafter on lettering, wood engraving, and satirical cartoons. He considered himself in debt to Eric Gill for "showing him the way," and remained active with the Ditchling community until being forced to retire by poor health in 1957. He produced most of his work to order, and no editions of his prints were made during his lifetime.

Hagreen's work was very wide-ranging, ranging from such small items as the bookplate for the "Eric Gill Collection" of his friend, George Bernard Shaw, to the illustrations used in the literary series, *The Best Poems Of*, published in 1922, 1923, and 1924, and selected by Thomas Moult.

Other Hagreen illustrations appeared in William Adlington's *The Golden Ass of Lucius Apuleius* (1924), René Le Sage's *The Devil on Two Sticks* (1927), W.A. Woodward's *The Countryman's Jewel* (1934), Lady Strachey's *Nursery Lyrics and Other Verses for Children* (1922) and Fr. Casimir Kucharek's *The Byzantine Slav Liturgy of St. John Chrysostom* (1974). In 1933, he illustrated and introduced *Silversmithing: Its Principles and Practice in Small Workshops*, by fellow Guild member, Dunstan Pruden. Still more of his work can be found in *Meditations on Our Lady*, *Apostles' Calendar*, and *The Countryman's Jewel: Days in the Life of a Sixteenth Century Squire*; collections of his work include *Philip Hagreen: The Artist and His Work* and *The Ex-Libris of Philip Hagreen*.

Hagreen was also a pithy and penetrating writer, who contributed regularly to *The Cross and the Plough*, the journal of the English Catholic Land Movement, edited by Harold Robbins from 1934 to 1946. He also wrote frequently for *The Sign*. Towards the end of his rather long life, he wrote *The Artist and His Work* (1975), where he sought to sum up his artistic experiences.

S. SAGAR

"S." Sagar is one of the great "mystery men" of the second generation of Distributists, who followed in the footsteps of Chesterton, Belloc, McNabb, and others. Those few still alive (as of Summer 2008) who knew him, such as Aidan Mackey, only ever knew him as "Mr. Sagar," and his full Christian name continues to elude discovery. Hailing from Lancashire, he was an extremely prolific writer whose interests were wide: Distributism, religion, culture, politics and agriculture. All of these were subjects which he wrote upon regularly and with zest.

In the 1930s, Sagar wrote regularly for the *New English Weekly* (*NEW*), set up in 1932 by A. R. Orage and edited, following his death, by Anglo-Catholic Philip Mairet, who had lived for a time at the Ditchling of Gill and Pepler, and was also a member of the Kinship in Husbandry and (thanks to the encouragement of T. S. Eliot) Maurice Reckitt's Christian Social Movement. Sagar's work for the *NEW* revealed his sympathy for the organic and ruralist ideas of both H. J. Massingham and Viscount Lymington.

Towards the end of the 1930s, Sagar appears to have begun writing exclusively for *The Weekly Review* under Hilary Pepler and Reginald Jebb. His articles were often a page or less in length, but they were meaty in content and pithy in style.

Sagar's six-part *Weekly Review* series, "Distributism," was reprinted as *Distributism* in the 1940's and again in 1990 by Distributist Books. The series was widely read; Dorothy Day, for instance, quoted from it for her *Catholic Worker* newspaper. He also wrote *Round by Repentance Tower*, a 1930 book published by Sheed & Ward of London, subtitled "A Study of Carlyle."

VISCOUNT LYMINGTON (1898–1984)

GERARD VERNON WALLOP, the Viscount Lymington, became the 9th Earl of Portsmouth early in 1943, upon the death of his father, Oliver. He was born in Chicago and raised in the United States, where his parents had a farm near Sheridan, Wyoming. He was educated in England at Farnborough, Winchester College, and Balliol College, Oxford. In 1923 he took over a 150-acre farm on a family estate. As a farmer and landowner he was, according to Dr. Philip Conford, "successful and progressive."

He served as Conservative MP for Basingstoke (1929–34) and was a leading member of the English Mistery, founded in 1931 by William Sanderson, before splitting with him in 1937 to form the back-to-the-land "English Array." The Array's journal was the *Quarterly Gazette*, and the movement was dedicated to, as Lymington put it, the regeneration of the English stock and soil; opposition to alien corruption, internationalism, and usury; craftsmanship and domestic responsibility; and the employment of organic agricultural methods to replenish the soil and produce healthy food. While leading the Array, he founded an additional journal, the *New Pioneer*, whereupon he collaborated with John Warburton Beckett (an ex-socialist MP), A. K. Chesterton, Anthony Ludovici, Philip Mairet and others; he was also its editor from 1938 to 1940.

In the face of the increasing likelihood of war in Europe, he founded (also in 1938) the British Council Against European Commitments, while Array activities ceased in 1940. He also joined the British People's

Party, and collaborated in the foundation, with Rolf Gardiner, of the Kinship in Husbandry–of which he was, with Gardiner, effectively the heart. It was an informal but influential alliance of ruralists, whose aim was, according to Drs. Richard Moore-Colyer and Conford, to restore the English yeomanry, establish local and regional self-sufficiency, resurrect the craft tradition, and repopulate the English countryside. The group included as members other figures such as H.J. Massingham, Philip Mairet, and Adrian Bell, and it influenced other organicist and ruralist organizations such as the Rural Reconstruction Association of A.J. Penty and Montague Fordham and the well-known Soil Association. He was also a member of the Council for Church and Countryside, founded by David Peck and Reverend Patrick McLaughlin.

His books include *Horn, Hoof and Corn*, *Ich Dien: The Tory Path*, *Famine in England* (at the time a *Sunday Times* "book of the month"), *Alternative to Death*, and *A Knot of Roots*, his 1965 autobiography. He contributed to Massingham's 1945 anthology *The Natural Order* and wrote for John Middleton Murry's paper, *The Adelphi*. After the war he settled in Kenya, where he was eventually to own about ten thousand acres of land, and where he would remain for about 25 years. He served there as member of the Board of Agriculture, chairman and later president of the Electors' Union, and member for agriculture of the Legislative Assembly, which latter post he maintained for three and a half years, beginning in 1957. In 1965 he was invited by Jomo Kenyatta to become a special advisor to the Ministry of Agriculture, Fisheries, and Food. He held the post until 1976, when he suffered a stroke and returned to England. Speaking of the Lymington legacy, Conford notes that he was "crucially important in development of the organic movement."

About IHS Press

IHS Press believes that the key to the restoration of Catholic Society is the recovery and the implementation of the wisdom our Fathers in the Faith possessed so fully less than a century ago. At a time when numerous ideologies were competing for supremacy, these men articulated, with precision and vigor, and *without* apology or compromise, the only genuine alternative to the then- (and still-) prevailing currents of thought: value-free and yet bureaucratic "progressivism" on the one hand, and the rehashed, *laissez-faire* free-for-all of "conservatism" on the other. That alternative is the Social Teaching of the Catholic Church.

Catholic Social Teaching offers the solutions to the political, economic, and social problems that plague modern society; problems that stem from the false principles of the Reformation, Renaissance, and Revolution, and which are exacerbated by the industrialization and the secularization of society that has continued for several centuries. Defending, explaining, and applying this Teaching was the business of the great Social Catholics of last century. Unfortunately, much of their work is today both unknown and unavailable.

Thus, IHS Press was founded in September of 2001A.D. as the only publisher dedicated exclusively to the Social Teaching of the Church, helping Catholics of the third millennium pick up where those of last century left off. IHS Press is committed to recovering, and *helping others to rediscover*, the valuable works of the Catholic economists, historians, and social critics. To that end, IHS Press is in the business of issuing critical editions of works on society, politics, and economics by writers, thinkers, and men of action such as Hilaire Belloc, Gilbert Chesterton, Arthur Penty, Fr. Vincent McNabb, Fr. Denis Fahey, Jean Ousset, Amintore Fanfani, George O'Brien, and others, making the wisdom they contain available to the current generation.

It is the aim of IHS Press to issue these vitally important works in high-quality volumes and at reasonable prices, to enable the widest possible audience to acquire, enjoy, and benefit from them. Such an undertaking cannot be maintained without the support of generous benefactors. With that in mind, IHS Press was constituted as a not-for-profit corporation which is exempt from federal tax according to Section 501(c)(3) of the United States Internal Revenue Code. Donations to IHS Press are, therefore, tax deductible, and are especially welcome to support its continued operation, and to help it with the publication of new titles and the more widespread dissemination of those already in print.

IHS PRESS ◆ Non est enim potestas nisi a Deo ◆

For more information, contact us at:

mail: 222 W. 21st St., Suite F-122~Norfolk, VA 23517 USA
toll-free telephone or fax: 877-IHS-PRES (877.447.7737)
e-mail: order@ihspress.com • *internet:* www.ihspress.com

IHS Press is a tax-exempt 501(c)(3) corporation; EIN: 54-2057581.
Applicable documentation is available upon request.